Creating a Healthier Church

CREATIVE PASTORAL CARE AND COUNSELING SERIES
Howard W. Stone, Editor

CREATING A HEALTHIER CHURCH

Family Systems Theory,
Leadership,
and Congregational Life

Ronald W. Richardson

FORTRESS PRESS
MINNEAPOLIS

CREATING A HEALTHIER CHURCH
Family Systems Theory, Leadership, and Congregational Life

Scripture quotations unless otherwise noted are from the Revised Standard Version of the Bible, copyright © 1946, 1952, 1971 by the Division of Christian Education of the National Council of Churches of Christ. Used by permission.

Cover design: Brad Norr
Cover photograph: Reverend Elayne Lipp. The photo was taken at a congregational retreat of Messiah Evangelical Lutheran Church, Minneapolis, MN.

Library of Congress Cataloging-in-Publication Data

Richardson, Ronald W. (Ronald Wayne), 1939–
    Creating a healthier church : family systems theory, leadership,
and congregational life / Ronald W. Richardson.
        p. cm.
    Includes bibliographical references.
    ISBN 0-8006-2955-8 (alk. paper)
    1. Church management. 2. Christian leadership. 3. Family
psychotherapy. I. Title.
BV652.R56 1996
250—dc20   96-6369
                                                              CIP

The paper used in this publication meets the minimum requirements of American National Standards for Information Sciences—Permanence of Paper for Printed Library Materials, ANSI Z329.48-1984.   ∞

Manufactured in the U.S.A.   AF 1-2955

00   99   6   7   8   9   10

CONTENTS

FOREWORD

If you are interested in learning how the parish, as a system, functions, you are in for a treat. If you are interested in your parish system flourishing, then *Creating a Healthier Church* by Ron Richardson is not to be missed.

Creating a Healthier Church is written not only for parish pastors, but for other members in the congregation who serve as church school teachers, administrators, board members, choir directors, and so forth. All of these people, because of their significant roles in the parish, are a part of the total leadership of the church and are key members of the system known as church.

Creating a Healthier Church examines the church systems we find ourselves in and constructs strategies for bettering them. First, it describes systems theory to help readers understand how parish churches work and how problems can develop in them. Second, it suggests ways in which ministers and other leaders can act when caught in a maelstrom of conflict in a parish. Third, it provides a practical set of ideas that leaders in the church can use to address common problems encountered in the parish. And finally, the book provides church leaders with specific ways they can enhance their own leadership abilities.

A key concept in the book is *the church as emotional system.* Richardson contends that within every parish system are a variety of other systems and sub-systems. He lists examples of such systems as the structural, communication, decision-making, economic, and cultural. One of the most important systems within each church is the emotional system. He describes it as "one of the most powerful forces in any church or in any group of human beings. The health of the emotional system determines how well the other systems work. A poorly functioning emotional system will derail the best and most rational planning efforts." He then goes on to help readers assess the emotional system that operates in their own congregations.

I found the last chapter on leadership one of the most fascinating in the entire book. Here Richardson describes how each of us as leaders can review our own style of leadership so that we will function as better leaders in congregations.

Richardson has included questions at the end of each chapter to assist leaders in the church to assess what is happening in their congregation and discuss changes that might be instituted to help make the congregation healthier.

I have followed the ministry of Ron Richardson for over twenty years and have been impressed with the sensitive way he performed parish ministry, the skill he used in pastoral counseling, and the knowledge he has about family systems applied to the church system. This is an admirable book and I anticipate it will have an impact on the church for many years.

Howard W. Stone

ACKNOWLEDGMENTS

I want to thank the late Dr. Murray Bowen and all of his colleagues at Georgetown University and the Georgetown Family Center for developing family systems theory to help us to better understand human beings in community. I thank those who have worked with me here in Vancouver over the last 20 years for being a community in which my own thinking could develop. And I thank Lois, my wife of 29 years. She was able to live the principles in this book before we knew there was such a thing as family systems theory. She has taught me more about being a self in relationship than any theory could. And she has lovingly given of herself, her time, and her editorial skills to make this book more readable.

1

INTRODUCTION
WHEN BAD THINGS HAPPEN
IN GOOD CHURCHES

For while there is jealousy and strife among you, are you not . . . behaving like ordinary [people]?   *(1 Corinthians 3:3)*

Strive for peace with all men [and women] . . . that no "root of bitterness" spring up and cause trouble.   *(Hebrews 12:14-15)*

A SUNDAY MORNING IN TWO CHURCHES

Following are the stories of how two different churches reacted to the same situations encountered on a Sunday morning. As you read the stories, be aware of what was different in each church and think about what might have happened in your church. Note in particular the behavior of the leaders.

Third Church

Early on a cold, blustery Sunday morning in December, the phone rings at Andy White's house. Andy, the building committee chairperson of Third Church, answers the phone knowing that a call at this time of morning probably means a problem of some kind at the church. He hears the custodian, Wayne Higby say, "Andy, I've got bad news. I've just arrived at the church, the heat is off again, and I can't get the boiler started. It looks like it has been off most of the night and the temperature inside is about forty-five degrees."

Andy groans, thinking about how this will affect the morning. Church school is scheduled to begin in about an hour, and the worship service will begin an hour after that. Even if the boiler magically started now, it would take more than two hours to heat up Third Church's huge sanctuary to a comfortable level.

11

As Andy thinks about these things, Wayne continues. "But that's not the worst of it, Andy. I think something's happened in the sewers. With all that sleet and the snow melt yesterday, about two inches of sewer water have backed up into the day-care rooms and it smells to high heaven all over the basement."

"Oh, no! That's awful," Andy responds, greatly understating his feelings. Anything else you have to tell me, Wayne?"

"No," sighs Wayne. "I just thought I'd be spending the morning getting the ice off the front steps, but I'm confused now about where to start."

"Right, the stairs have to be done too," Andy agrees. "How does this sound? Call the boiler repair service and ask them to come as soon as possible. Then you can start on the steps. I'll call the pastor and let him know what's happening. Maybe he will be willing to call Susan [the day-care director] and see if she can take charge of the basement situation."

"Great," says Wayne. Andy ends the call by promising to be at the church in about thirty minutes.

Next, Andy calls Bob Stimson, the pastor at Third Church, and fills him in on what is happening and what the plan is. Bob says he'll think about what kind of adjustments he can make to shorten the worship service and let people go home earlier, and he offers to call Susan.

Before heading down to the church, Bob calls Susan Azur, the day-care director. Her agency rents space from the church. Susan is horrified by what has happened, thinking of the twenty children who sleep and play on that floor every day. She wonders how the center can possibly open up in less than twenty-four hours, "if ever again."

But once Susan calms down, she asks Bob what she can do, and he suggests that she try to find an emergency cleaning service to come in. After the obvious health issues involved, his next thought is about the cost of the clean-up. He knows the church budget is tight, and he figures Susan's budget is too, but he raises the possibility that she might have access to some emergency United Way money to help pay for this kind of thing. They agree to do their best to split the costs of the clean-up.

When Bob gets to the church that morning, Janice Hoppe, the church school superintendent, tells him that things have been "a bit of a frazzle" for her that morning, also. Three of her eight teachers called in sick, and she had to find substitutes. But the kids seem to be enjoying having class in their coats and hats and mittens, and, while not enthusiastic about the cold rooms, the teachers decided to work both the cold and the powerful odor into their Advent lessons, reminding the children that Mary and Joseph didn't have warm houses to go home to when it got cold, that Jesus was born in a cold and smelly cow barn, and so forth.

During the worship service, with the radiator pipes banging away loudly in the sanctuary as the heat came up, and with the clean-up men starting their pumps and yelling at each other just outside the building and in the hallways, Andy is glad that Bob has decided to shorten the service even more. Andy also thinks that Bob does a good job when, during the announcements, he tells the congregation of the morning's events and got some chuckles, especially from the older members of the congregation who learned long ago not to expect perfection in life. Bob is pleased with their response and privately gives thanks that, for the sake of time, it is not a Communion morning.

But there are two infant baptisms to do. The older of the two babies begins crying as soon as he takes her into his arms (as Bob knew she would because of her age). The neck microphone amplifies her wails throughout the building. With all the activity and confusion, no one is monitoring the volume on the amplifier, so the congregation has to endure some powerful screams as the baby bellows out her alarm over the stranger holding her. Mary Doyle, the worship committee chair, is finally able to get to the amplifier and turn it down.

The younger baby plays her part with all the cuteness that one could expect, making her parents proud and adding some warmth to the service. But she has a thoroughly wet diaper and Bob smiles to himself thinking his "sprinkling" of her was meagre compared to her own liberal contribution.

After the service, as people leave, they express a good deal of understanding for what things had been like that morning. Some members compliment Bob on the "brevity" of his sermon ("Maybe we should keep the heat off all the time," one person mused); others talk of "the good old days" when there was never much heat in the sanctuary; Miss Jones says it is too bad he'd had them sing only one verse of her favorite hymn; and various other members remind him that it has been a while since he called on this or that shut-in. He thanks each of them for the reminder and says that the shut-in is "lucky to have a friend like you."

Bob then has a quick discussion with Mary Doyle, the worship committee chair, about plans for the Christmas services. One point of disagreement on the committee has been whether to use live goats and sheep in the Christmas pageant or not. What does Bob think?

Bob and Andy speak about how the morning is progressing. They are both satisfied with how the difficulties are being handled. Then they go to the adult class, which is officially a "talk back" session where people freely offer their comments on the service or the sermon. As could be predicted, Joe Thompson has some negative things to say about Bob's "liberal politics" in the sermon, but Joe's comments lead to a fruitful discussion, with people asking Joe thoughtful questions about his position and expressing some of their own thoughts about the sermon, which happened to touch on abortion.

Bob always finds this class to be a valuable experience, as he gets to hear more about how some of his members think about their life and the world. He seldom feels the need to, and rarely does, defend his own positions. Without appearing to "grill" them, or be defensive, he often asks questions of the class members that have the dual effect of helping him to understand them better and helping them think through more completely their own opinions and experience. Nearly everyone in the class finds this useful and marvels that they can talk about "potentially divisive issues" without a lot of hostility and still have their different points of view, even learning something in the process.

On the way out, Bob talks with Andy again about the building problem, who is doing what, and what still needs to be done. They congratulate one another for dealing well with a difficult situation.

When they each finally get home for a late lunch, they tell their wives that it hasn't been such a bad day; while they don't want to go through another one like it, they are impressed with people's ability to be flexible, to adapt to the situation, and to be clear about what is important in the church. Both Andy and Bob are happy to be part of this church.

Valley View Church

By a very strange coincidence, almost exactly the same events transpire that same Sunday morning just two miles away at Valley View Church. But matters progress in a different way and have quite a different outcome.

Building committee chair Stu McGuire gets the phone call from the custodian, Larry Lambert. Larry starts by saying, "Mister, you better get down here real soon. You've got a big mess on your hands here. The heat is off again and the sewer has backed up into the day-care playroom. There are two inches of muck on the floor, and it smells worse than a garbage dump. And don't expect me to clean it up! I can't work in these conditions. I especially don't want to go out and clean slush and ice off the front steps if I can't come in and get warm. What are you going to do about this mess?"

Knowing that Larry could go on for another twenty minutes like this, Stu interrupts him. "Hold on, Larry, hold on! Did you press the red restart button on the boiler like I told you to do last time?"

Larry retorts, "You know I don't like to fool with that thing. Are you trying to get me blown up?"

Stu interrupts again, saying, "You won't get blown up. I've explained this to you a thousand times. I don't want to have to come all the way down there just to start the boiler."

Stu, angry again that the pastor has hired Larry over his objections because Larry was an out-of-work nephew of a committee member, wonders how to stop Larry from being so helpless. The only technique he has found to get any action at all is to keep giving Larry the occasional kick. So, operating on this theory, he continues, "You know, I've told you, too, to keep those sewer drains cleaner; that mess in the basement is probably your fault. You've got time today to clean off a little bit of the snow and ice on the stairs and then start cleaning up the day-care floor. I'll talk with the pastor and have him call Anne and tell her she has to do something about her rug. Now get busy!" Stu hangs up.

Then he calls the pastor, Roy Hanson. As soon as Roy says hello, Stu jumps in. "Roy, you know how I've been saying the boiler needs to be serviced and you guys never listen to me. Well, now it's gone off again during the night. I sure wish you and the committee would be willing to spend a little more money to look after things. Now I'm going to have to take all the complaints from everyone this morning. It's forty-five degrees in the sanctuary and Larry won't even try the restart button. I don't want to have to go down there just to push the restart button, and I figured you must be going over there soon and you can do it. Right?"

But Roy argues, "Look, Stu, I keep telling you people the church didn't hire me to be a boiler mechanic. Dealing with the boiler is your job. And anyway, I'll be the one getting all of the complaints.

I've got the whole worship service and two baptisms to do this morning, and you want me to deal with the darn boiler. Where are your priorities?"

Stu responds angrily: "Well, you've got a bigger problem. The sewers have backed up into the day-care playroom, and there is muck everywhere. I'm sure it's another thing that Larry has been doing wrong. And since it's your fault that he's our custodian, I guess you'll have to call Anne Whalley."

At this, Roy blows up. "Right! Along with everything else I've got to do this morning. Boy, you are something else. I don't know why I have to do any of this, but it sure seems like I'm the only one who ever does anything around here. None of you people ever seem to know what my job really is here, and I end up doing all of yours. Goodbye!"

After he hangs up, Roy knows he shouldn't have spoken that way to Stu, but all the frustrations of dealing with that committee and the roadblocks they keep putting in the way of his efforts to have a better functioning plant just came to the surface. It kind of surprises him, but he doesn't seem to have any control over it. Anyway, it feels good to let out some of this frustration. He hopes Stu gets the point. Roy proceeds to complain to his wife, Joy, about how they are trying to take advantage of him again. Joy just tries to keep calm and not say anything, because she is upset with how Roy talked to Stu. She thinks that the church might try to get rid of Roy, and he doesn't seem to realize that is a possibility. Since her own job is not that secure, she is worried.

When Stu's wife, Lolly, sees Stu's face turn red as he talks with the pastor, she knew they are in for another one of those bad days at the church, which had become fairly common. She listens as Stu calls some of his committee members and tells them briefly about the problems at the church and, with more feeling and in greater detail, about how the pastor has gone off on another one of "his royal rampages" about church members and how nobody but him ever does any work around there.

Stu and these friends agree that the church would be a lot better off without this particular pastor. But then, the quality of pastors generally seems to have declined over the years anyway. The last three pastoral relationships at Valley View, before Roy, ended unhappily, with the turmoil centered around the pastor. Members blame it on the general decline in the quality of denominational leadership and of teaching in the seminaries.

Lolly also calls a few of her friends that morning, telling them her version of her husband's version of the phone call with Roy Hanson that morning. They all agree that this is getting to be typical of the pastor, even though "he seemed to be such a nice man when he first came here." Each tells more negative stories about him, some of which are old and well-known stories and some of which are new. This leads to a discussion about Roy's wife. Some of Lolly's friends think she is part of the problem and is not "a proper pastor's wife." Others defend her, saying, "Look what she has to live with. She doesn't seem too excited about him either."

By the time people get to church that morning, many of them were already expecting the worst from Roy. Face to face with him, they are polite but distant. Some are especially warm to Joy. They say it is a "difficult morning" and tell her some of the things "others" are saying about Roy, which they knew must be hard on her. Joy responds with a facial expression that some of the women interpreted as a "you don't know the half of it" kind of look.

When Roy calls the day-care director and tells her about the situation and that she has to do something about it at her expense, she gets angry. She rejoins that he and the church board are very uncooperative, that the church has been a poor host to their agency, and that she has been talking to another church about moving her day-care program there. As far as she is concerned, the rent is supposed to take care of situations like this, it is the church's building, not hers, and this church doesn't seem to have a very strong commitment to Christian ministry in the community. She says she will get a clean-up crew, but the church will have to pay for it. Roy manages to restrain himself from saying all of what he feels like saying and just mutters, "Fine, go find another church to take advantage of," and hangs up.

When Roy gets to the church that morning, the church school superintendent, Maureen Niven, presents him with her resignation. She explains that she spent the whole morning trying to find substitutes for those teachers who had "just decided they couldn't make it this morning." She was already fed up when she walked into the building that morning, but the cold and the stench are the last straw for her. She can't run a proper church school in these kind of conditions and with no support.

She reports church school attendance has been low for a long time, that people are blaming her for this, and that she just doesn't need any more of this kind of criticism. All of her teachers and volunteers agree that the problem is not with her. She "knows" that the problem is really with the curriculum, which both the teachers and the children hate, but which is being shoved down their throats by the denomination and by Roy.

Roy doesn't say anything, but he is steaming under his white collar. He goes to his office, closes the door, and stays there until it is time to start the service. He sits there thinking about how badly he has been treated in this church, how misunderstood he is, and how something is going sour in the church. Deep down, he feels somewhat guilty and thinks that he should be different somehow, but as soon as he begins to have these feelings and thoughts, he starts to remember all the times church members have mistreated him, and then he says to himself, "It's just not my fault."

During the announcements and the sermon that morning, Roy's anger comes out in his references to a "lay leadership crisis" in the congregation and a need for "more dedicated members" who understand "the true meaning of the church and feel a call to serve others in a spirit of love rather than backbiting." He sees certain people squirm when he says these things and tells himself he is right on target and that they needed to hear this.

During the first baptism, the baby screams into Roy's neck microphone. The worship committee chairperson, Harry Harding, who is sitting in the choir, scribbles a note and drops it over the choir stall railing onto the pastor's chair. During the last hymn, Roy reads the note: "When are you going to get someone to be responsible for the sound system? I've told you how upsetting this is to people in the congregation. Either they can't hear a thing, or we have this kind of racket going on. We must not have another Sunday morning like this. Do something!"

During the not very happy "greeting" time at the door following the service, someone mentions a shut-in who needs visiting, and Roy snaps, "I'll get there when I have time." He then goes to talk to Harry, almost waving the note in Harry's face, demanding to know where he ever got the idea that the public address system is Roy's responsibility, that this was the worship committee's job, and that, again, he can't be responsible for everything in the church.

In this mood, Roy goes into the adult class, which immediately becomes hushed as he walks in the door. The group has been having a barely disguised conversation about the pros and cons of the pastor's personality.

The class has never been a successful "talk back" because as soon as people say what they think, Roy defends his sermon and repeats it all over again, telling them they don't understand what he was saying. So the class leader will usually try to identify a theme from the morning and ask people to talk about their experience with this theme in their own lives. But quite regularly, and this morning is no exception, the conversation moves back to what the pastor said, and Roy gets defensive. The class ends with the leader saying something like, "Well, I'm sure we will continue this discussion for a long time to come."

Before leaving the building, Roy and Stu have another confrontation in which each blames the morning's problems on the other and justifies his own behavior. Both go home without knowing exactly what is happening about the building and who is doing what next.

At his late lunch, Roy complains to Joy about all that has gone wrong and how ungrateful people are. Joy is worried about Roy's future with the church, and since other people's problems with him are similar to her own problems with him, she begins to tell him some of the things she heard about him that morning. Joy thinks it works better if she uses other people's words, rather than her own.

There is, however, a bit of an accusatory tone to her voice, and in reaction Roy begins to tell her how even she doesn't understand him and that she doesn't do enough either to defend him to others or to support him in this difficult congregation. Joy stops talking at that point. They finish lunch in a hostile silence, with each feeling uncared for by the other.

WHAT THIS BOOK IS ABOUT

How can we account for the differences in what happened in these two congregations on the same Sunday morning in the same kind of circumstances? Both congregations come from essentially the same geographic, socioeconomic, ethnic, cultural, and educational background. Yet the two congregations reacted very differently in response to the same events.

At Valley View, it would be easy to focus solely on Stu McGuire, the building committee chair, or on Roy Hanson, the pastor, or on a couple of other "problem" people in the congregation, and to point to their obvious mistakes and poor handling of the situation. While I have intentionally exaggerated the reactions and specific words used at Valley View and condensed a lot of experiences into one Sunday morning, each of these things has been said and done by well-meaning and good Christian people at different churches.

We all know that in marriages that are going badly, it is rarely just one person's fault; both people have a part to play in the problems. The same thing is true in congregations. All of the members, and especially the leaders of a church, contribute to whether things go in a more positive or negative direction.

So what is going on when a church gets into some of the difficulties Valley View has and the leadership seems to be making things worse rather than helping to provide a positive direction? And how can we account for the fact that things go well at Third Church and the leaders are able to avoid the emotional outbursts and turmoil common at Valley View? What is it about our human nature, about our strengths and liabilities as people, and about the way we organize ourselves in groups that make things go well or poorly when we are faced with problems?

This book will address those questions and offer you, as a concerned member and leader in the church, the following resources:

1. a theory about human behavior that will help you understand how things can get out of control in the human community of the church and turn out as they did at Valley View;

2. a practical set of leadership ideas and behaviors that can prevent things from going that way and have them turn out more like they did at Third Church;

3. some guidelines for how to behave in the midst of upsetting and conflictual circumstances in the church, when things do seem to be going as they did at Valley View;

4. and some personal steps that you, as a leader in the church, can take so that you can become a more positive force for healing and cooperation to develop a healthier church community.

WHO THIS BOOK IS FOR

This book is for anyone who has any kind of leadership or decision-making role in the church. It is not just for the "top leaders," those on the governing board, clergy, and denominational leaders. It is for committee members, administrators, church school teachers, custodians, secretaries, librarians, choir directors, organists, and Sunday morning "greeters" and ushers. All of these people, by virtue of their roles and positions in the church, are an important part in the whole matrix of church leadership.

If you have one of these roles, you may not think of yourself as a "leader," but that is what you are. You contribute to the tone or atmosphere of church life, not only as an individual personality but as part of a collective group spirit.

No one at Valley View intended for things to go as they did that Sunday morning. They each felt caught in something that was not of their making, and they tried to handle it as best as they knew how. Without thinking about it, they fell into an automatic way of relating that only seemed to make things worse.

This book will present questions at the end of each chapter to help you think about the concepts being discussed and how they might apply to you and to your own church. To get the most benefit from your reading, you might want to discuss the material in this book in a small group, with the committee you work with, with other members of your board, or in whatever grouping of people in your church would make sense to you. The questions are intended to help you each think about your own church experience. There is no need for the group to agree or to arrive at a consensus. There are no correct answers.

This book is meant as a tool to help you think about your own way of being in the church and how you function in relation to others. A cartoon depicts a man standing in front of two racks of books in a book store. One rack is full of books and is labeled "Self-Help." The other rack, nearly empty, is labeled "Other-Help." Often we are tempted to read self-help books with an eye to how they apply to others rather than to ourselves, as if they were really "other-help" books. I hope you can avoid this temptation. You will gain the most value and positive results if each of you read this book to learn how it applies to yourself.

As each of you, as church members and leaders, reflects on your own role in the church and how you have dealt with challenges in the church in the past and how you would like to deal with them in the future, you will automatically begin to behave differently. You will be creating a healthier church community that can support growth and healing in each individual member and better accomplish its mission in the world.

THE THEORETICAL BASIS OF THE BOOK

This book is based on an approach to understanding human beings variously called natural systems theory, Bowen theory, or family systems theory. Murray Bowen, the originator of the theory, was a professor of psychiatry in the School of Medicine at Georgetown University in Washington, D.C. He died in 1990. He was one of the innovators in the field of family therapy, which began to emerge in the 1950s. His theory is a milestone in ways of working in family therapy and in understanding human relationships generally.

A few family therapists began to discover that the concepts Bowen developed applied not only to themselves and their own families and the families they worked with in therapy but to their work setting and to organizations generally. I first discovered this when clients began to report that the therapy we did in relation to their families had an impact on how they performed in their workplace and volunteer settings and that those aspects of their life were getting better as a result.

In 1986, I began to offer courses for clergy based on Family Systems Theory (FST), and clergy began to report a revolution in their own thinking about problems in the parish and their own role in relation to these problems. These clergy in turn began to wish there were some kind of tool for helping their church members benefit from FST.

So this book is based on my:

- understanding of family systems theory;
- work as a trainer and clinical supervisor of students learning to become marriage and family therapists;
- ten years as a parish pastor before I trained to become a pastoral counselor;
- clients' experiences as they have tried out, with many positive results, this way of thinking in their own work settings and churches;
- work with over eighty parish clergy and church staff members who have taken the eight-month course, "Using Family Systems Theory in Your Ministry";
- experience as the executive director of a nonprofit pastoral counseling agency with thirty clinical staff; and

- work as an organizational consultant to churches and secular work groups.

This book is not about the one correct way for leaders to lead. There are many ways to implement the concepts given here and many routes to the same goal of a healthier, better functioning church community. Ultimately, each church, each leader, and each church member will do it in his or her own way.

2

THE CONGREGATION
MORE THAN MEETS THE EYE

". . . visiting the iniquities of the fathers upon the children to the third and fourth generation. . . ."   *(Exodus 20:5)*

There are many parts, yet one body.   *(1 Corinthians 12:20)*

A NEW WAY TO THINK ABOUT
HUMAN BEINGS AND RELATIONSHIPS

Think for a moment about the way things went on that Sunday morning at the two churches. What interactions reveal the strengths in one and the liabilities in the other? How do you explain these to yourself? How do you think you would have behaved in the same circumstances, especially if you were in Valley View church and had the sort of encounters with others that they did? How would you have tried to exercise leadership and express your Christian ministry to one another in that setting?

Every act of ministry, exercise of leadership, or way of relating to others in the church comes from an underlying belief, or theory, about how human beings function. We make assumptions about what motivates others and guides their functioning, about how they create problems for themselves, and about the resources they have for dealing with difficult situations.

Third Church and Valley View clearly have different ideas about what makes people tick and what motivates them. They have different (though unconscious) theories about human behavior. At Valley View, other people are perceived as threatening, and each person is on guard from potential attack by another. This comes out most clearly in the exchanges between Stu McGuire and the church custodian, Larry Lambert, but it is present in the other exchanges as well. People also keep trying to shift the responsibility (or blame) to others. Like Adam and Eve in the garden trying to explain why they ate the forbidden fruit, everyone tries to place the "blame" for what happened elsewhere.

At Third Church, however, Bob Stimson and the members seem to believe that they are all in it together—that everyone will do their best to make things work. Responsibility is automatically shared, with each person doing his or her part. No one has to be pushed, blamed, made to feel guilty, or "motivated" into behaving in a responsible way.

The basic difference in the two unspoken theories about human behavior is that the people at Valley View have an "individual" model and the people at Third Church have a "systems" model of human beings.

In the individual model, there is little sense of people's interconnectedness or of how one's own behavior can affect that of others. People are seen as acting on their own, as though in a vacuum. Who they are as individuals is understood on the basis of their "insides," their own biological, psychological, and moral being. This leads to seeing particular people as "the problem." No one includes himself or herself as a part of the problem. Each person feels blameless and sees other individuals as the problem. It is hard to imagine any of the folks at Valley View believing "we are all in this together."

In the systems model, there is recognition of the connections between people. It says that people can only be understood fully within the context of their relationships. No one lives or acts in isolation, and we are all affected by each other's behavior.

These theories about human behavior are usually not talked about or even thought about consciously. Few people at either church may be aware that this is how they think, but their functioning is evidence of their underlying thoughts about humans. Outwardly, both churches in their worship service that morning may have recited the Apostles' Creed and affirmed the importance of loving their neighbor, but how they behaved with each other as a Christian community was quite different. Verbally they both professed the same faith, but behaviorally they had a significantly different faith.

This is not to say that people at Valley View were not sincere in their faith or did not intend to live a Christian life. They were and they did. But in the midst of difficult circumstances, they acted on the basis of their unconscious theories about human behavior. They got caught up in an emotional process that kept them from being able to express their faith behaviorally.

At Third Church, faith and practice came closer together. Leadership was expressed more effectively, and ministry was engaged in because of the sense of connection and shared responsibility. No one felt accused or attacked or put down—or needed to evade his or her own responsibility. And no one was singled out as "the problem" or the only one who should take responsibility. Everyone involved talked and dealt with one another in a respectful way. Individuals took responsibility for their own part and yet functioned cooperatively in relation to each other. Each one could give and take guidance, teach and learn from one another. There seemed to be a balance of individual responsibility and community awareness, concern, and connection.

As a result, Third Church was able to get on with its mission in the larger world in a more focused and effective way. Their church life was not a hindrance to their mission. They were highly cooperative and competent in seeking to be Christ's body in the world.

Valley View was a more self-centered church, spending much more time and energy on its own internal problems. It had little left to give to the larger world.

NO ONE IS AN ISLAND

One of the keys to functioning in a healthy manner as a church is for the leaders to look at the church as a system rather than as a collection of isolated people. Every church is more than a collection of individual members. People in the church, as in any group, are intricately interconnected. They exist in a system that is much bigger and more powerful than the individual members. Each person both influences and is influenced by everyone else.

Even though each person has individual strengths and liabilities, those attributes can change in different contexts or relationships. This is frequently illustrated in marital therapy when a business executive says, "What's going on with me? At work I communicate well; I work well with those above and below me; I stay calm in tense situations and think clearly and make good decisions. But as soon as I get home and my partner complains to me about something I did or didn't do, I become a basket case. I act like a rebellious teenager, just like I did with my parents."

The same person, in two different contexts, or systems, has two different ways of reacting in emotional situations. Looking at this from a systems perspective reveals that this person functions differently in these two systems of work and family. These different ways of being help to account for the different personality styles shown in the two systems. The larger systems can affect the expression of individual personality.

Thinking systemically is very difficult. Roy Hanson couldn't see how his own behavior affected those around him, and the church members couldn't see how their actions affected Roy and each other. When things start to go wrong, it's easy to see how others are behaving incorrectly and how they impact us, but it's difficult to see our own part in what is happening, and how we impact others.

The relationship between Stu and Larry the custodian won't get any better until at least one of them can get some perspective on his own role in their interaction. No doubt Larry complains to his uncle on the building committee or to the pastor about how Stu treats him unfairly, just as Stu complains to his wife about how "dumb" Larry is. Neither one thinks about how his behavior affects the other or about how the larger situation contributes to the emotional intensity of their interactions.

At Third Church, each person's ability to remain relatively calm as the difficulties develop helps others stay calm. Members are able to stay more connected with one another and be more cooperative and thoughtful as they decide what to do. In both churches, the system responds to and is created by the actions of the individuals and vice versa.

In the church, each member functions in relation to each other member in that system. Member's functioning may be different or similar to the way each person functions in other systems (family, work, and the like). We develop our identity as church members and leaders in relation to the identity of others in the church. And the church as a whole develops a collective identity in relation to other systems—other churches and the community. When people talk about particular churches, they often ask, "What kind of a church is it?" This question recognizes that each church takes on a particular personality over the years.

The identity of individuals and of the church also develops in relation to previous generations of church members. In the Bible, this is recognized in passages like "visiting the iniquity of the parents upon the children, even unto the third and fourth generations" (and, I would add, visiting the blessings, as at Third Church). One young pastor was told by her bishop, "This church you're going to begin serving destroys their pastors. They're demanding and hard to please. You'll have to be tough with them." She was then hard-nosed and rigid in a way she would not normally have been and, of course, got into trouble with the congregation.

What the bishop did not recognize when he later tried to come to her rescue and failed was how he was a part of the system himself. Although he was trying to be supportive of her, he set her up for a fight with the congregation. This church's personality had developed within a particular context that almost everyone was oblivious to, but that context had a strong impact on pastor-church relationships. So particular churches develop a way of functioning within the larger system (in this case the diocese), just as particular church members develop their roles within the church system. And the past functioning of all the systems affects the present.

Each church member, past and present, affects every other church member, whether there is direct contact between them or not. Decisions made by a committee of people whom the church school teachers have never met (either in the church or at the denominational level) can still have a big impact on what gets taught in the church school. Maureen Niven, the church school superintendent at Valley View, was reacting in part to this outside influence when she resigned.

Each person does not affect, and is not affected by, others to an equal extent. Some members carry more weight or are more influential than others. A missions committee chair who doesn't like denominational policies about the poor can sway the board so that the congregation never hears about a new program to aid poor people, even though the members would have been willing to support it.

Change in one member in a congregation can affect the whole. Most often the change in that one member has been preceded by changes in others. The system is the total of all the members and their different actions and reactions.

What happens in the life of a church when a key, active member dies or moves to another church? Or what happens when the perennially sought for "new blood" does show up and then wants to do things differently? (This often provokes the "Seven Last Words of the Church" response: "We never did it that way before.") Think what it is like for you when you go to a church meeting or event and only a few of your old friends are there, but many new people are there. You might be saying to yourself, "It's just not the same." All of this is part of the church system.

And this church system is just one of many systems that we all belong to and that affect each other. A bad day at the office (the work system) can lead to a bad night at home (the family system). Roy Hanson's relationships with congregational members are influenced by his relationship with his wife, his denominational executives, his pastor colleagues in other churches, his friends, and most importantly his family of origin—the family he grew up in.

This book will not deal with the impact of our family of origin on our adult life and relationships. However, this impact is a major emphasis of Bowen's family systems theory, and any effort to look at this part of our lives will make a significant contribution to our efforts to change ourselves as adults. If you wish to pursue this aspect of the work you might read the author's book on family of origin work, *Family Ties That Bind* (Self Counsel Press, 1984).

SYSTEMS WITHIN SYSTEMS

Within the church system are a variety of other systems and subsystems. Some of these include the cultural, the structural (who has what offices and performs what jobs), communication, decision-making, and economic systems. Each of these is relatively obvious, rational, and easy to talk about and change, if necessary. Churches often have planning retreats focused on improving these systems.

However, it is the emotional system that is the most difficult to detect and to understand, let alone to try to change. The emotional system is one of the most powerful forces in any church or in any group of human beings. The health of the emotional system determines how well the other systems work. A poorly functioning emotional system will derail the best and most rational planning efforts.

It is essential that leaders in a church be aware of how the emotional system operates in their own congregation. They need to be aware of the part they play in the emotional system and how they can become a more constructive force for improving the emotional life of the church. One of the main ways Valley View is different from Third Church is the degree to which Valley View is controlled by a less functional emotional system.

Emotional systems are like delicately balanced mobiles. Any movement by any one part of the mobile, toward or away from the center of gravity, affects the balance of the whole mobile. This is most true of the parts closest to the top of the mobile (the leadership), and only somewhat less true of the parts closer to the bottom. As soon as a mobile gets out of balance and hangs askew, it needs to be rebalanced to hang properly.

There will always be times of imbalance in the church's emotional system, times when there are conflicts and problems in the church that challenge the leadership. That is normal and unavoidable. But how these situations turn out—and whether they are ultimately experienced positively or negatively—is what makes your church more like Third or like Valley View. And this depends primarily on the actions and reactions of the church leadership—the lay leaders and the clergy and other professional church staff.

When the emotional system becomes unbalanced, the response of church leaders is crucial to how things turn out in the end. During times of imbalance, church leaders often become the target of people's anger in the church, on matters great and small. If the leaders think in individualistic terms rather than in systems terms, they are likely to respond to attacks as though they personally were being attacked, rather than seeing the attack as part of an imbalance in the system. If they think this way, however they respond, whatever they actually do or say, more problems will result and church life will become more chaotic.

Leaders or not, everyone is involved in the emotional system, but some people are controlled by it more than others. The more rational and thoughtful we can be in the midst of emotional turmoil, the less vulnerable we are to the power of the emotional system.

The people at Third Church could experience the same level of emotional upset as those at Valley View, but they were able to be more objective about the situation and their reactions. They were aware of their feelings, but they did not have to act simply on the basis of those subjective feelings. They could have their feelings, rather than their feelings having them. They were able to think about the situation and what would be the most helpful thing to do, rather than react emotionally.

At Valley View, the reactive feelings took over. People got stuck in their emotionality and had trouble moving beyond it to deal with the situation at hand. A difficult situation was made worse by their emotional reactions. This is a natural human response to stress or the experience of threat.

A good way to see the emotional system in action is to watch how various churches and their leadership deal with controversial issues. One current issue for many denominations is whether or not to ordain homosexuals to the ministry. In Canada, the United Church decided to do this. Each congregation had its own unique reaction to this and dealt with this denominational decision differently. Some congregations were able to manage themselves well in the midst of the emotional turmoil that resulted, and others came apart at the seams.

The emotional system is no respecter of politics. It does not correspond to either "liberal" or "conservative" beliefs. Some people in the United Church, in both liberal and conservative churches, went off the wall emotionally, saying they would leave the church if it either did, or did not, pass the resolution. Leaving the denomination was not the main indicator of their being taken over by the emotional system. It was the amount of emotionality they displayed in the process.

Many members were upset, regardless of which side they were on, but they were able to maintain a more or less reasonable connection with those on the other side. A few members were concerned about the issue and passionately invested in a particular outcome, but they did not get emotionally reactive about it (again regardless of which side they were on). They argued strongly for their own position but respected other people's positions and beliefs. They learned from and maintained a friendly relationship with their opponents, without compromising their own beliefs.

IN THE EMOTIONAL SYSTEM, RELATIONSHIPS ARE NOT WHAT THEY SEEM

One Sunday morning at Valley View Church, the women's association president, Marie Fontana, asked to talk to Roy in private. In Roy's office, she told him that she was upset with Harry Harding because he and his worship committee had ignored the women's association request not to move the flowers on Sunday morning. That morning, Harry had moved the flowers to the side of the sanctuary. She also said that her committee was upset with the worship committee's plan to remove the flags from the sanctuary.

Roy told her that he "frankly" also found Harry a difficult person to work with and "not very co-operative." (Roy knew he shouldn't have said this, but he wanted to show support for Marie.) He said he would talk to the worship committee and see what he could do about the flowers. He did not tell her that he was really behind the effort to remove the flags from the sanctuary.

Marie said how much she appreciated him, that she knew he was having a hard time in the church, and that she was willing to be there for him as a "sounding board." He then told her that he thought people dumped on him and that the church lacked good leaders who were willing to take responsibility, like she was. They wanted him to do everything.

Marie sighed sympathetically and said she knew what he meant. She said she also felt misunderstood by almost everyone, including her own husband. At this point, she began to cry and Roy hugged her, which she appreciated.

In this situation, Roy sees an opportunity to develop an ally in the church, and Marie sees an opportunity to get some help with her goals. They both appreciate getting some sympathy and emotional support. The threat exists that an even closer relationship will develop between them, due partly to the nature of their connections and way of functioning in the larger emotional system. Generally, we would think of this relationship as just two people getting involved, as in the diagram below:

FIGURE 1

But this dyadic relationship is not simply about just these two people coming together. It includes the emotional system, the whole mobile, of the church and all the other mobiles of which they each are a part. For Marie, this includes other women in the women's association; members of the worship committee she feels at odds with; her unresponsive husband; her practically grown, somewhat hostile children; her infirm mother (alone since Marie's father died at an early age); and her unmarried younger brother. Here is a graph of these relationships in Marie's emotional system:

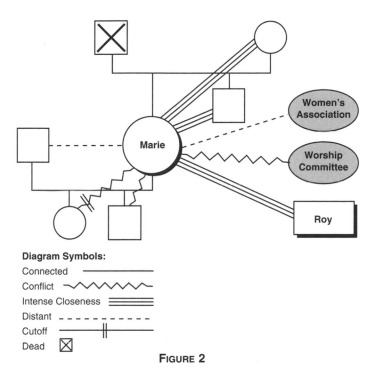

Diagram Symbols:
Connected	———————
Conflict	∿∿∿∿∿
Intense Closeness	═══════
Distant	- - - - - - -
Cutoff	——‖——
Dead	⊠

FIGURE 2

Roy's mobiles include the congregation of Valley View; his clergy colleagues in the denomination, who he thinks are against him; his wife and two daughters, who seem to have little appreciation for him; his alcoholic father; his mother who looks after everyone but herself; and his favored older brother, a successful doctor. Here is a graph of his emotional system:

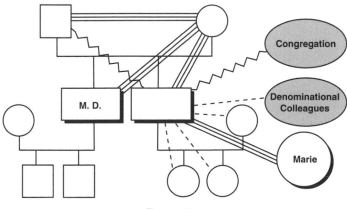

FIGURE 3

When Roy and Marie come together, a crowd of other people are also present emotionally. The electricity between the two of them gets its charge from each of the separate, larger emotional systems which each of them is a part. From their different, unstable mobiles, they are each reaching out in the hope of finding some stability with each other.

When family systems therapists do marital therapy, they look at the life and context of both parties in much the same way. They do not see just two individuals; they see parts of a mobile of relationships. By looking at all the mobiles, therapists can better understand the behavior of the couple and begin to think about what change will involve.

This emotional system is present no matter what the connection between two people. For example, two copastors involved in a team ministry also bring their individual mobiles into their copastor relationship. David and Wilma work well with each other in every area of church life except finances. When they get into heated discussions about the church budget, they start to label each other's behavior in negative ways. He calls her "cheap" and "overly cautious." He says, "You have to be willing to take risks and incur debt to get a good payoff. Even if we have an unbalanced budget this year, we'll have more money coming in next year if we invest in this more expensive program."

She, on the other hand, says he is "irresponsible" with money and takes too many risks and that the church will run out of money if they do things his way.

It goes on and on in a discussion they have many times over, with neither of them changing their position. Both can quote Scripture that they believe supports their own positions.

What makes their job of finding common ground more difficult is the way they begin to personalize each other's position and put negative labels on each other. This helps lock each of them in their own position.

What they don't realize is how many other people from their lives are in the room with them and how earlier experiences in other mobiles have shaped them. Here is what their discussion about this topic actually involves:

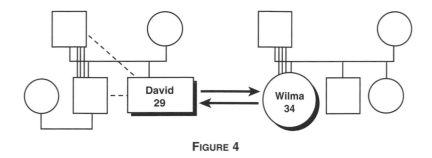

FIGURE 4

David is a younger brother of a brother (who tend to be greater risk takers generally). His parents and his older brother live very conservative lives financially, and it seems to him that this is getting them nowhere. Wilma, on the other hand, is a very responsible eldest child who worried about financial security in her family partly because her father (who happened to be a youngest) went bankrupt three times in risky ventures. She thought she was the one who held things together during these times in the family.

Any discussion about money between David and Wilma is bound to involve for each of them their past experiences with money in their families. They probably won't be aware of the influence of these earlier experiences, which makes the experiences even more powerful. David and Wilma are not likely to make much headway with each other until they realize how much their current attitudes about money are affected by their earlier family experiences. The emotional system (the mobile) of their two families of origin have bumped into each other in the emotional system of their work mobile.

Whether or not David and Wilma ever agree on the church budget, the same kind of clashing of emotional systems will take place among board members when they meet to discuss the budget. The various mobiles of each board member will be present, too.

Here is a graph of a church board (or committee) attempting to deal with a difficult issue like money. The church board members are within the inner circle; the individual emotional systems that they bring to the meeting lurk just outside the circle.

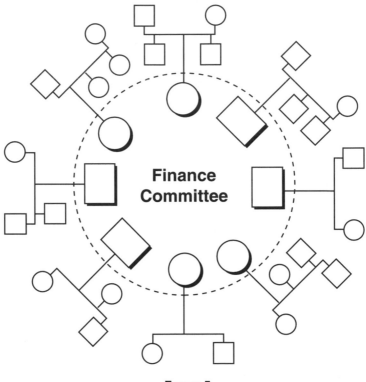

FIGURE 5

It can be overwhelming to think of the church as a place where all of these mobiles (not just individuals) come together. But this is a fairly accurate picture of what is happening and helps to explain the tremendous complexity of church life and the emotionally powerful experiences people have there.

We all come into the church with a huge number of important connections, which, if ignored, make church life more difficult and less satisfying. Effective church leaders recognize the reality of these larger emotional systems for themselves and others and look at what happens in the church from this perspective.

IMAGINATION AND FACT:
LEARNING TO OBSERVE THE EMOTIONAL SYSTEM

A primary skill for learning about how to deal with your congregational emotional system is the ability to be a good observer.

Observation requires stepping outside of our own subjective responses to what we "feel" is happening, and learning to watch what is actually going on: who is doing what, when, where, and how.

Many of us spend a good deal of our time living in a kind of fantasy about what is going on around us. We observe a few things that happen "out there," fail to see or even ignore other things, and create a story for ourselves explaining what it is all about. We might think of ourselves as good observers, but in fact most of us are not. We go right from a few pieces of observational data into our beliefs about what is going on and why people are doing what they do.

The individual model of human behavior leads us to speculate about other people's inner motives—and to try to assess whether their motives are "good" or "bad." Nobody really knows about other people's inner motives and intents (we often don't even understand ourselves in this area), so we do a lot of imagining or develop a "fantasy" about what is going on with others when they do what they do. In our most subjective moments, we begin to believe that we even know them better than they know themselves.

But most often our beliefs about the reasons others do what they do have more to do with our own subjective experience of their behavior and how it impacts us. How we assess them depends on whether we feel good or bad in response to their actions. That is the nature of subjectivity. Then we react to what we imagine they are doing "to us" (or to others), and they then react, in the same way, to our reactions. This is what happened at Valley View repeatedly (where there was a lot of second guessing about people's motives). This keeps an emotional system in turmoil.

For example, Stu was convinced that Larry was simply an irresponsible, lazy man who had no ambitions in life and whose only goal was to do as little as possible. Acting on this "belief" about Larry's motives led Stu to behave in certain ways, to which Larry then reacted in a predictable way, and around it went, each reacting to the other's reactions.

No one ever achieves total objectivity or can get completely outside of this reactive cycle. No one ever gets totally outside of his or her own emotional system. But any movement toward becoming more objective within the system, by even one person, will be an asset both to the individual person and to the system.

Objectivity requires paying attention to the "functional facts" of the emotional system and not speculating about things we can't see or don't understand (such as motives). Functional facts are described as we answer questions about the who, what, where, when, and how of behaviors, not the why.

For example, in the midst of a committee discussion, one member may seem to respond to a comment of ours with a raised eyebrow, then look down, and become silent. These are functional facts. Just as I describe this scenario it is almost automatic within us to go beyond these facts and to begin to assume what is going on with the person (for example, he or she is angry, sad, fearful, and so forth).

We could assume any number of things about this behavior and ascribe a "reason" to it. And then we begin to behave toward the other as if the explanation that we have imagined is what is actually going on with the other. Our imagined reason for the other's behavior could be self-blame ("I made him unhappy by what I said") or other blame ("She refuses to talk this out with me and is going to fight me with silence"). The reality is more likely to be like an actual explanation I heard once: The quiet person was asked about his behavior and said he had forgotten to do an errand for his partner and was thinking about that, not about what had been said.

This demonstrates another element of subjectivity: We tend to personalize other people's behaviors. We think the behavior is about us. We think someone is reacting to us, when in fact, as above, he or she isn't thinking about us at all. Even if that man's quietness is about something you said, his reaction to it could be more about him than about you. And you wouldn't know anything about the "why" of that until he felt comfortable enough to tell you about it.

Jesus commented once (speaking of the Holy Spirit) that the wind blows where it wills, and we may not know much about why it does this, but we can observe the effect. In the same way, the forces at work inside people are often beyond our understanding. The workings of the emotional system within each individual person are not yet well understood. But we can pay attention to how people relate to one another. What are the functional positions that people take in relation to one another?

As we learn to become good observers of the emotional system at work in our congregation and of who does what, when, where, and how, then we can even learn to predict what might come next. Accurate observation will lead to a certain amount of predictability, which then allows us to begin to think and plan about how we want to be within the system when certain upsets happen, so that we can be a resource to the system rather than contribute to the turmoil through our own subjective reactions.

This skill also requires that we learn to become good observers of ourselves within the emotional system. Achieving a more objective stance means we can think more clearly about our own subjectivity and about how we get caught up in the emotional system and thus trigger our own reactivity.

QUESTIONS

For Your Own Thinking

1. Think of a couple of problems or difficulties you have had in various relationships recently, situations in which someone else has behaved in a way you didn't want him or her to.

- How do you explain to yourself this behavior and the difficulties between the two of you?
- Do you tend to understand the difficulties as all the other person's fault or all your fault?
- If you removed the idea of "fault" from your understanding of the behavior, then how would you understand the difficulties in the relationship?
- Do you know what you have to do to get the unwanted behavior from the other? If so, what?
- If you can think of it this way, what would be your "best" technique for getting this unwanted behavior from the other?
- To what extent do you insist that the only thing that can make the relationship better is for the other person to change?

2. What do you think you learned in your own family of origin about human nature and motivations?

- What did your parents actually say to you about "people" and about "you" in particular? What do you think they believed, based only on their actions towards you and others?
- What did you do with these "teachings" from them over the years of your growing up?
- How have they affected your own beliefs about human nature and motivation?
- In what way does your faith challenge or affect these beliefs?

3. To what extent is the idea of "an emotional system" a new one

to you, and how well does this idea fit with your own understanding of relationships in the church?

• Think of an example of the emotional system at work in your church.

• Think of times when the emotional system within the congregation undercut the goals and planning efforts of the church.

4. Think of ways your relationships with and experience in your family of origin, or in your present family (if you are married or have children), have affected how you relate to the church or particular issues or concerns you have in the church.

5. As an exercise, try drawing your own family diagram (similar to those of Roy and Marie on page 33) and then ask yourself, In each of these relationships, how does the idea of "church" or my actual involvement in the church affect this relationship?

6. If you have been on a committee or board of the church, think about whether you have ever found yourself taking a position or voting a particular way, because of an experience with family or friends? For example, when issues of money are discussed, how does your own experience of money in your family affect your position in the church?

For Group Discussion

1. Discuss in your group any questions or comments you each have about chapter 2.

2. If you would like to, share with the group any thoughts you had in response to the individual questions above.

3. What are some recent "unbalancing" events in your congregation, and how did you see people deal with the experience?

4. How well does your congregation deal with "controversial" issues?

• What helps or hinders this?

• How do you see your own abilities in this area?

5. Describe a recent upsetting event in your congregation in purely functional terms, only addressing questions of who, where, what, when, how, and ignoring the question of why.

• How does this way of describing the event affect your understanding of it?

• To what extent do you find this useful?

6. What biblical stories and theological themes seem relevant to what is discussed in this chapter?

3

WHAT UNBALANCES
THE SYSTEM?

"Do not be anxious about your life."   (*Matthew* 6:25)

For God did not give us a spirit of [fear] but a spirit of power and love and self-control.   (*2 Timothy* 1:7)

WHAT IS ANXIETY?

The intertwining mobiles that make up the emotional system of the church can easily get out of balance. Both the stimulus for the unbalance and the unbalancing itself can be experienced by some people as a threat. These people then react to the perceived threat in ways that create more unbalance, which then creates an even greater sense of threat within the system. In humans, the innate biological response to threat is either fight or flight. Our automatic reaction is to react aggressively and attack or to run away in fear.

One way people differ from one another lies in how much sense of threat they carry around with them, versus how safe they feel in the world. Each of the people we met at Valley View lives with a higher sense of threat than those we met at Third Church. Larry, the custodian, experienced threat right away when he went into the church building that Sunday morning and knew that he was going to get blamed for and have to take care of the messes. He tried to deal with this aggressively (fight mode) in his phone call to Stu McGuire, the building committee chair. Stu also immediately sensed a variety of threats in the situation and also chose to deal with the threats aggressively, first with Larry and later with the pastor. Stu's aggression was in turn experienced as a threat by others who either counterattacked or disappeared.

At Third Church, people generally have a lower sense of threat so they react differently to situations that others might see as threatening. They don't add their own internal level of perceived threat to the reality of difficult situations, and thus they don't make a situation even more upsetting. They deal with "what is," rather than with what they imagine.

Andy White, the building committee chair, felt a sense of threat pass over him when the custodian called him with the bad news. But he dealt with it quickly by focusing on the reality of the situation. He did not have to attack Wayne, shift the blame, feel guilty himself, or ask why this was happening to him. He just had to think clearly about the next step to take.

Susan Azur, the day-care director, also felt a bit threatened at first, but she also quickly recovered and was able to work with the pastor on pursuing a course of action. Other members reacted similarly as the morning progressed. To the extent that there was any sense of threat in people at Third Church, they did not get caught up in it, and the threat didn't keep them from doing reasonable and cooperative problem solving. Because they didn't feel personally threatened, they didn't need to waste time being angry and blaming others.

Whenever people feel threatened or under attack, as they did at Valley View, the emotional system begins to get out of control. The threat may not even appear particularly dangerous. It could just be a feeling people have when they are not getting what they wanted or expected from others, their life, or the church. The attack or threat does not have to be intentional. The decision to move the flags out of the sanctuary at Valley View was not meant as an attack on people. But many took it this way. The sense of being under attack often has to do with people's perceptions, which are based on their life experience over many years. They tend to interpret present-day experiences in terms of those historical experiences. Because these historical experiences (particularly those in our family of origin) are so powerful for all of us, they tend to control our current functioning.

Family systems theory calls the sense of threat that people, or systems, experience "anxiety." Anxiety in this sense is different from the phenomenon of panic attacks, where people are hit suddenly with dramatic symptoms that make them think they are having a heart attack or other imminent crisis. Anxiety *can* be experienced in ways that make its presence unmistakable to us. But most of our everyday, or chronic, anxiety happens beyond our awareness, so that we are not conscious of how much it controls our functioning. It is this kind of anxiety that swept through the people of Valley View Church on that cold December morning. But if you had asked them if they were "anxious," very few would have said yes. They might have reported other feelings, such as anger, hurt, fear, or sadness. But probably no one would have called what they were experiencing anxiety.

Anxiety is a very uncomfortable feeling. It is more uncomfortable than fear, which is a reaction to the known. Knowing what we are afraid of gives us some sense of control. The control we usually have in fearful situations is to stay away or avoid the situation. If we are afraid of snakes, heights, closed places, angry people, or whatever, we can avoid the feared thing by keeping our distance. This ability to distance provides us with at least some sense of control for ourselves.

Anxiety is less tangible and more amorphous than fear. For this reason, we feel a lack of control. For example, when people have suffered from vague physical symptoms that doctors cannot diagnose, they feel anxious. But once the cause of the symptoms is determined, their anxiety often decreases. Even if a serious disease is diagnosed, they often feel some relief because it is a specific problem that they can work on. Their anxiety was a result of being out of control and not knowing what was going on.

Churches, like individuals, differ in the level of chronic anxiety they experience. A few churches have such a high level of anxiety that they verge on being paranoid. They see everything as threatening. Some churches feel completely safe in the world and do not see anything as a serious threat. Most churches experience some threats and vary in how anxious they feel or how safe they feel in the world.

The churches that function the best have leaders who experience less threat around the normal unbalancing that occurs (acute anxiety) and feel safer in the midst of the erratic movement of the mobile, while staying in touch with all parts of the mobile. The closer to the top of the mobile these calmer leaders are, the greater the calming effect they will have on the whole congregation. The more threatened and unsafe the leaders feel generally (chronic anxiety), the more the whole congregation can be disrupted.

The leaders may not always be those in designated official positions. At Third Church, the members who showed up for worship to find the heat off and who laughed it off and shared their lightness with others were leaders. They had no official office in the church, but they automatically made a positive and constructive contribution to the life of the church that morning. Whatever their ability to behave in ways we typically associate with "leadership," those who bring a lower level of threat or anxiety and a higher level of personal safety, while remaining connected to others, become "leaders" in the church.

The threats that can provoke anxiety can either be real or imagined, but they may be just as powerful in either case. The physical situation at both churches was a real threat to the peace, enjoyment, and comfort of the Sunday morning service and a threat to the health of the children in the day-care center. This kind of threat can provoke acute anxiety. Acute anxiety is a reaction to specific situations that are challenging, outside of our normal daily experience, and in need of some kind of focused attention from us. In themselves, most people can manage in situations of acute anxiety.

How well acute anxiety is managed often depends on the level of chronic anxiety within individuals and in the emotional system. So the negative reaction to the Sunday morning situation was much greater at Valley View partly because of the ongoing high level of chronic anxiety there; it was a church already "on the edge." Some were reacting not only to the actual threat but to imagined threats. For example, Larry, the custodian at Valley View, had a very active imagination about what the mess meant for him or about how pushing the restart button on the boiler might cause an explosion. Some people, because of their general level of unhappiness with the church, made it into a bigger deal than it was. Then, as the level of anxiety increased throughout the congregation, the level of reactivity increased as well.

HOW ANXIETY DEVELOPS IN HUMANS

Theory of Abandonment

John Bowlby, a British researcher and psychotherapist, has taught the world a great deal about anxiety. In *Attachment and Loss*, he wrote about what happens when infants are physically separated from their mother. It can be a threatening and even terrifying experience. The infants use various psychological mechanisms to cope with it.

Essentially, we learn from Bowlby that the origin of anxiety is a complex perceptual/physiological/emotional experience. The infant perceives a threat in the physical separation from mother. This perception of threat leads to the production of various hormones that stimulate the infant physically and emotionally. The infant then gives a sound of alarm (crying). The cry is an effort to regain the sense of support/nurture/protection that the infant feels when in contact with mother. Every mammal species, including humans, has this kind of mechanism for dealing with the separation/threat experience. We all recognize the crying of an infant who is unwillingly separated from the parent, whatever the animal species involved.

Human infants start off life totally dependent on parents to provide for vital needs. The human physiological/psychological wiring is built so that infants keep track of the nurturing and protective parent as much as possible through touch, sight, and sound. When that parent figure is missing, the infant feels vulnerable, and perhaps unsafe or threatened, and then becomes anxious.

Bowlby observed infants crawling on the floor near their mothers. Following their natural desire to explore new things, they would crawl some distance away from mother but look back at her at some point and make visual contact with her. If everything seemed okay, they kept crawling around, making occasional eye checks on mother's presence.

At some point in their wanderings, the infants would crawl back to mother and make physical contact with her, sort of verifying that she was really there and everything was all right. Then they would wander away again to explore some other part of the room. Eventually they might wander into the next room, but they kept looking back around the corner from time to time to make sure mother was still there. At some point, they returned again physically to touch home base. Mother's constant presence, and the ability to have access to her and make contact with her, helped the infants feel safe enough to go out and explore on their own.

When mothers disappeared from the room or if a stranger was placed between mother and the infant, a degree of alarm was noticeable on the infant's face. The infants began to feel unsafe and at some point began crying. This reaction was most common in infants who were from six to eighteen months old. That's how Bob Stimson knew that the first baby was going to cry when he took her in his arms for the baptism (she was eleven months old) and that the younger one would be able to handle a stranger's face looking down at her (she was four months old).

As children get older, they can tolerate greater periods of separation from the caretaking parent without feeling unsafe. They have learned from experience that "out of sight" is not "out of mind" and that the parent can be counted on to be there at the appropriate times or if there is a need. Each extended separation and reunion teaches the child that separation and distance from the parent is not always threatening. At the same time, the child is learning that she or he is increasingly okay and capable when the parent is away.

Part of what allows the child to tolerate longer separations is that the child begins to introject, or psychologically take into his or her sense of self, the caretaking parent. Enough reliable experiences of separations and reunions create the idea of a safe home base that is carried around psychologically in the child's head, and the need for actual connection is reduced.

Also, the parents own level of safety and anxiety affect the infant. Infants can "catch" the calmness or anxiety of a parent. The response of a parent to a situation can teach the child whether or not it is a threat. For example, the look of alarm on a parent's face can stimulate a fearful reaction in the child.

In family systems theory, it is understood that the child's attachment is not really just with a primary caregiver, usually the mother, but with the whole emotional system that the mother is a part of. If mother is more securely connected within her emotional system and feeling safe within it, the infant experiences her as a safer home base. If she feels anxious about her connection to other emotionally important adults, this can affect the nature of the connection she has with the child. The general level of safety versus threat that exists in the whole family system is inherited by the child as his or her level of chronic anxiety.

Eventually, in normal development, the child discovers that he or she can manage long periods of time out of the caretaking parent's presence and still feel okay. The first day of day care, kindergarten, or school, is a marker of this transition, which can stimulate anxiety in both parents, as well as the child. Then the child can spend overnights at a friend's home, go away for weekends, or go away to camp for a week and know that home and parents will still be there. As these repetitions of separations and reunions continue, the idea of home as a safe and reliable base and the child's own developing sense of mastery are integrated into the child's psychological experience. A child then can spend lots of time out in the world, maybe even at great distances from home, and maintain a sense of safety.

Ideally, by the time most people reach young adulthood, they discover that they have most of the emotional resources they need within themselves to be on their own without feeling too overwhelmed by life. They have a sense of safety and self-support and are less anxious as adults. If this normal process has been interfered with for any number of reasons, the young adult will have a higher level of chronic anxiety and feel more easily threatened by life events and relationships.

Emotional Skills Development

Just as children develop a sense of safety or threat in relation to important family members, they also develop or fail to develop skills that contribute to their sense of self-support, or competence, in life. Some things they learn from parents and other adults, some from their own friends, and some things they discover for themselves.

Many skills are openly taught and learned; others are learned only by observation. Skill in dealing with emotional issues is usually unconsciously learned by observation. We learn emotional skills by observing how family members deal with their own emotions, especially in upsetting situations. We tend to develop levels of emotional skill similar to those of the adults in the family. For example, if you grew up in an environment where people felt anxious and were uncomfortable dealing with anger and conflict, you would have a higher level of chronic anxiety that would make it very difficult for you to be around an angry person. Your typical response might be avoidance or flight, without ever addressing and resolving the issues between you.

Emotional skill (or lack of skill) is rarely something of which we are aware. One night early in their marriage, Pastor Bob Stimson and his wife, Alice, had just gone to bed. Their bedroom door and the windows were closed and the lights were off. Just as Bob was falling asleep, Alice said with some urgency, "Bob, there's something flying around in here." He said, "Don't be silly. What could be flying around? Go to sleep." But she insisted something was flying and told him to listen. He did, and heard a barely audible "whoosh, whoosh, whoosh."

Immediately, he felt the same alarm Alice did. They both pulled the covers over their heads. They were experiencing acute anxiety: a sense of threat, no sense of self-support, and lack of safety. What made it different from simple fear was that they didn't know exactly what it was they were afraid of.

Finally, Bob slipped out of bed and crawled across the floor to the light switch. When he turned on the light, he saw that it was a bat flying around the room. Alice felt both vindicated and more frightened. Bob, however, calmed right down. Saying, "Oh, it's just a bat," he ran downstairs and came back with a broom and some newspaper. He calmly knocked the bat down and held it to the floor with the broom while he folded the newspaper around it. He took the bat outside, let it go, and then came back to bed just like this was something he did every day, when in fact he had never done it before in his life.

Alice, amazed, asked him how he had known what to do. He said he didn't know. But then he remembered when he was about seven he had seen his grandmother do the same thing. She had done it calmly, like it was nothing to be concerned about. Although he hadn't consciously remembered this event out of his history, he immediately knew how to deal with a bat in the house. This "skill" was stored away in his brain to be called upon as an act of self-support in just such a situation. He not only remembered the technique, he also remembered that it was nothing to get upset about.

Until he knew what he was dealing with, he was as anxious as Alice. But once he discovered what the situation was and that he had the ability to deal with it, he again felt safe and competent. If his grandmother had reacted in terror to the bat in her house, Bob might still be hiding in the bed. His unconscious memory of her technical and emotional skills enabled him to react helpfully and appropriately as an adult.

The more practical and emotional competence people have, the greater their sense of safety and their ability to handle situations of acute anxiety. The less sense of emotional competence they have, the higher their level of chronic anxiety.

So learning how to deal with the mechanical reality of a broken boiler and a cold sanctuary or a bat in the house is one thing. Learning how to deal with the emotional reactions of yourself and others in the midst of situations like this is something completely different.

ANXIETY AND THE SELF

At its most basic level, anxiety is about the threat to the loss of who we are—our "self." At some preconscious, instinctual level, this is what the infant fears in the separation from the primary caregiver. Being so dependent, the infant needs that parent's presence in order to survive. Abandonment is the worst thing that could happen.

As adults, we may not be so physically dependent, but emotionally we can feel as though our survival depends on others. The emotional equivalents of abandonment might be, for some, the feelings of being uncared for, not respected, not accepted, not listened to, not taken seriously, and so forth. At a deep level, we think we will perish unless the important people in our lives provide what we think we need from them emotionally. If they don't, we feel threatened. Our sense of self is incomplete, or under attack. This is the underlying attitude that just about everybody at Valley View Church carried around with them.

The more sense of self we have and the more we experience ourselves as competent people, able to deal with the world's challenges, the less anxious we are. Anxiety increases when the sense of being a safe, secure, emotionally competent self is threatened; and when this happens, one way of dealing with the anxiety is to look for others to make it better for us.

ANXIETY AND RELATIONSHIPS

The general level of anxiety that we carry around as adults affects all our relationships. Even when it is no longer literally true that we will not survive if we are abandoned, it feels true emotionally. This is called "unresolved emotional attachment." We try to resolve this issue through contemporary adult relationships, which we unconsciously substitute for our relationships with the original family members. We keep trying to reduce our level of anxiety by reducing the chances for abandonment.

Anxiety is a powerful force in emotional relationships. If we are anxious because we fear an important person will "abandon" us, we may do whatever it takes to prevent that. A wife whose husband wants her to stay submissive (because of his anxiety) may inwardly believe that if she were to be herself and become more assertive, her husband would leave. So she may sacrifice being herself to avoid the feared abandonment, and instead, predictably, become depressed.

Anxiety generated by our unresolved emotional attachments affects social and business relationships, as well as personal ones. We can't avoid the emotional processes. In every setting, at some level we want others to help us feel more secure, calm, satisfied, happy, or whatever we think we need.

It is the perception of threat that leads to increased anxiety. At Valley View, the threats were based more on people's perceptions about the intentions of others than on the actual events or behaviors. Their imagined sense of threat was first stimulated, or set in motion, by the occasion of a "real" threat of a cold and polluted church building.

At Third Church the level of chronic anxiety was so low that the real threat did not unbalance it. The real threat, however, was enough to unbalance the mobile of a church as chronically anxious as Valley View. Valley View is so sensitive that any little wind blowing disturbs the balance. The wind could be any kind of change, not just an obvious problem. It could be the election of a new board, a large gift to the church endowment fund, or the arrival of a new pastor—or any of the changes and events, good or bad, that happen in a church's life on a daily basis.

A less anxious church may react to the wind blowing through the mobile by saying, "Wheee!" and finding it fun or maybe challenging. In the same wind, the more anxious church will batten down the hatches, convinced that all is lost and they are about to sink.

CALM LEADERSHIP IN THE MIDST OF ANXIETY

Anxiety, individually and collectively, is a powerful force for the church to understand and deal with. It can greatly interfere with our ability to be a faithful people of God. How things went on that Sunday morning at Valley View shows how anxiety can spread through an emotional system. One person's anxiety can trigger another person's anxiety, and this process can be multiplied many times over. The key for church leaders is to slow down this process before it gets out of control.

Electrical transformers function to increase or decrease the amount of power or voltage that is put into them. They enable you to plug a hair dryer into a 110-volt plug at one end, while 220 volts come out at the other end, and vice versa.

Some people and leaders in the church operate like transformers. They increase the voltage and generate even more electricity than was there to begin with, that is, they can increase the level of anxiety within the emotional system. This happened when Stu and Lolly at

Valley View began to call their friends; they were operating like anxiety generators in the system.

Other people operate in a way that decreases the level of anxiety; they tend to absorb it or dampen it so that the level of anxiety in the congregation is stepped down rather than up. Janice Hoppe, the church school superintendent at Third Church, did this with her teachers and with the students by her manner of dealing with the cold, smelly building.

The job of effective church leaders is to help keep down the level of anxiety in the emotional system of the congregation. When things are calmer, people are able to think more clearly about their options in the midst of stressful circumstances and develop a reasonable, workable plan of action. Effective leaders are able to help people manage their level of anxiety so they can accomplish these goals. They do this *primarily* by managing their own anxiety, and then, secondarily, by staying in meaningful contact with other key players in the situation. They do not tell others to "be calm." They simply bring their own calmness to the situation. By staying calm and yet connected to those who are anxious, these people help reduce the level of anxiety. People who do this are automatically positive and helpful leaders in the church, whether or not they hold an official office.

QUESTIONS

For Your Own Thinking

1. How anxious do you get when you simply think or talk about anxiety? What do you understand this to be about for you?

2. Think of some examples from your own childhood of how your anxiety was calmed by a parent's presence, or what it was like when you couldn't be with your parent (for example, when you were "lost" in the store).

3. Trace for yourself, psychologically, the development of a "safe home base." What events or markers along the way seemed to help it develop?

4. What do you consider to be some of the most valuable emotional skills you learned in your family? How do you think you learned these?

• Think of some specific examples.

• What are some of the emotional liabilities you learned in your family?

5. Do you think you tend to be a person who steps up the level of anxiety in your congregation or steps it down? Are you an absorber of anxiety or a generator of it?

6. What do you know about your own anxiety?

- On a scale of 1 to 100 (with 100 being the highest possible level of threat) what is the general level of threat in your life?
- When you do experience anxiety, how specifically does it manifest itself with you?
- What physical symptoms do you get when you are anxious? what emotional symptoms?
- What do you tend to do with this experience (or how do you deal with your anxiety)?
- How do those who are close to you respond to your expressions of anxiety?
- What responses from those around you seem to be most helpful to you? least helpful?
- How do you tend to respond to the anxiety of others?
- Are there any particular kinds of expression that you seem to have the most trouble with?
- How did your parents respond to your anxiety as a child?
- When you were a child, what kind of family situations would you tend to be anxious about?
- How did you deal with this experience?
- Have you changed the kinds of things you can become anxious about?
- How did you do this?
- What have you learned is an almost guaranteed way to make yourself anxious?

For Group Discussion

1. On a scale of 1 to 100 (with 100 being the highest possible sense of threat), what is the level of a "sense of threat" in your church? Please give reasons or examples of what leads you to give this rating.

2. What are some ways or times you have seen leaders in the church exercise some calming effect on the congregation's anxiety?

3. Have you ever seen someone manipulate a group of any kind by using the group's level of anxiety to get the group to do or be what the person wants? Give some examples?

4. When have you seen "change" (even if it is regarded as "good"

change) become a source of threat in the church? What useful resources were drawn upon by the people and the leaders to deal constructively with the change? When have you seen a failure to deal constructively with change?

5. What is the present state of your own congregational mobile? Is it balanced? If not, what is the degree of unbalance)?

• What are the "real" threats it is facing? What acute anxiety situations is it dealing with?

• How well do you think the church is dealing with this "threat"? Give some examples that support your point of view?

• What issues or experiences in the past remain unresolved in your congregation, contributing to the level of chronic anxiety and thus making it difficult to deal effectively with other, more immediate situations facing the church?

6. What are the positive qualities of anxiety? What might have happened in human history if God had not created us to be capable of anxiety? Where would we be without it?

7. What biblical stories or passages and theological themes address the issue of anxiety in our lives?

4

BEING ONE AMONG MANY

Then the LORD *God said, "It is not good that the man should be alone."* *(Genesis 2:18)*

". . . that they may be one even as we are one, I in them and thou in me, that they may become perfectly one." *(John 17:22-23)*

UNITY AND DIFFERENCES IN THE CHURCH

The New Testament authors, as did Jesus himself, regularly instruct us to pray, seek, and work for the unity of the church. But as the Book of Acts, the letters of Paul, and other New Testament writings show us so clearly, the early church had the same difficulties with unity that we do today. Then, as now, we keep coming up against the fact that our differences from one another are a stumbling block to our unity.

A dilemma about differences faces every person in every church: To what extent should I, will I, fit in and conform to the ways of this congregation, and to what extent can I, should I, be myself and follow my own path? Do I keep my differences to myself and appear to go along with others in the group because it seems to be "the Christian thing to do"? In many churches, being a Christian means not being allowed to be one's own self; it means behaving according to some stereotype of what a "true Christian" is. As a result, many of us think we have to check our identities at the church door, and while inside, we become something that we are not in the rest of our lives.

To some extent, and for each of us to a varying degree, differences in the church are not always a problem, and we can be understanding and accepting of them. But at some point, in every relationship and in every congregation, differences do become a problem. We can find them threatening and then feel anxious, and some of us find ourselves saying (perhaps only to ourselves), We are just *too different* from each other to be able to get along.

In some denominations, church officers and leaders are called "to study the peace and unity" of the church. The problem is that the way we usually understand "peace and unity" doesn't allow for the element of significant differences. If "peace and unity" means loss of identity and lack of conflict, then we will never be able to achieve this state in the church, and we as leaders are pursuing an impossible goal.

One group in the church will always believe one thing while another group believes something quite different. For example, at Valley View, some members believe the national flag belongs in the sanctuary, and another group doesn't; one group believes it is in charge of decorating the sanctuary for worship, and another group believes it is in charge. Difference and conflict are simply a part of what it means to be in a living human community, Christian or not.

When there is open difference and active conflict in the church, it often just doesn't "feel" right to us, and we tend to be uncomfortable, or anxious. Most often, a feeling of calm and satisfaction in the church coincides with a lack of deep differences being expressed and with people behaving similarly to one another. It's like when the choral anthem is sung particularly well, when the choir members sing their parts as written, stay together, and follow the choir director perfectly. The choral piece does have different parts. Not everyone sings the same part. But, on the other hand, the choir members don't sing simply what they want to sing. They still have to follow the part as written to create a "harmonious" experience.

The problem is, of course, that no one has written out all of the various parts for us to follow as church members and leaders in order to produce a harmonious church experience. We are each writing our own part as we go and performing it as best as we can, based on our understanding of what it means to be a Christian and an individual church member.

We often try to write parts for others by expecting them to behave and "perform" in certain ways in relation to our own part. But others frequently do not cooperate and end up "singing" something that is totally "off key" in relation to our own definition of what would be harmonious. They seem to be singing their own tune with the consequent effect (to our ears) of disharmony. Others also expect us to fulfill the parts they write for us in order to achieve their own version of harmony; for them, *we* are being unharmonious.

Thus the dilemma: Do we give up who we are in the church in order to appear to be unified, harmonious, and at peace with others, or do we openly say what we think, at the risk of being perceived as "troublemakers" within the community? As we look down that road of being individuals within the church, we ask how there can be peace and unity in the church if everyone is going to "do their own thing."

It's pretty clear that God did not create us all the same. Differences just go with being human beings. We seem to be created that way. In fact, ant colonies and bee hives are more "harmonious" than human communities. Many animals are able to achieve more cooperative and harmonious communities than do humans. What is our problem?

Theologically, we could say the problem is sin. And while this might be true, this answer can oversimplify the reality, and it doesn't suggest why some congregations are, in fact, more cooperative, more able than others to effectively set, pursue, and achieve mission goals and to create a harmonious communal life.

Family systems theory offers some concepts to explain how this dilemma comes about in human communities and what it takes for us to develop and to actively work for the peace and unity of the church, as people at Third Church did.

THE LIFE FORCES FOR TOGETHERNESS AND INDIVIDUALITY

Two deep and basic life forces are built into the biology of each human being and are at work in each human emotional system or community. These are the life forces for togetherness and for individuality.

These life forces are what give impetus or movement to life. They are what makes grass grow and flowers bloom, what pushes newborns to seek out the mother's breast, birds to migrate, animals (including humans) to both "congregate" and "individuate." Attraction and repulsion, competing and cooperating, loving and hating, pursuing and fleeing, dominating and submitting are all responses to these forces at work in our lives.

To a certain degree, our sense of self is strongly affected by the identities of the groups we are a part of: our marriage, family, workplace, school, social clubs or activity groups, favorite sport teams, town or city or nation, and, of course, our church. Each person gets some of his or her identity from the "togetherness" of belonging to a number of groups at particular levels of society. To belong, the individual person has to be willing to go along with the group, to fit in and be a team player, and to fulfill the expectations of the group— at least to a certain extent.

But our sense of self is also based on our own personal uniqueness or specialness. This is the individuality force. It is not about setting out to be different as a way of becoming distinctive; it is about thinking things through for ourselves and arriving at beliefs and understandings of our life and the world that make sense to us. This is something each individual person must do.

These two forces are at the core of the emotional system; they are the basic driving power of what makes life and relationships "go." They explain why we have this desire to be both "a team player" and "our own person." Socially and politically they lie behind the tension with which we regularly struggle: the rights of the individual versus the rights of the community.

The forces are not at opposite ends of a continuum, as if we can only be either "together" or "apart." The forces coexist within us, each force having varying levels of intensity at different points in time. The forces are not necessarily inimical to each other, and pursuing one will not necessarily mean we can't pursue the other.

But people at lower levels of emotional maturity often experience these two forces as polar opposites, creating the sometimes "torn" experiences of life where we want to go two directions at once. At this level, to be a part of the group appears to mean that we have to sacrifice our individuality, and to be an individual appears to mean we have to sacrifice community.

At higher levels of emotional maturity, we know more about how to keep these forces in balance within our lives, and we see situations less in terms of having to sacrifice either a part of ourselves or our connections with others. It is possible to be a self and to be well connected to others, but "it ain't easy"; it depends on our level of emotional maturity. This aspect will be explored in chapter 6.

The Togetherness Force

Togetherness is the biologically rooted life force that drives us to want to be connected to and affiliated with others. It is observed in every species of animal. It orients us to the group, or at least to those who are emotionally important to us. It is about our inevitable dependence on others and our need to be connected. It shows in our concern for others, our sensitivity to them, our ability to listen to them, to love them, and to both seek and give nurturing. And it is, for example, a part of what makes teamwork possible. It inspires us to seek "unity," in the church or in any other group we are a part of.

It is what drives parents to make extraordinary sacrifices for the sake of their children or for their families generally. It drives church members to give of their time, money, and energy to the work of the church and to make personal sacrifices on behalf of its mission and ministry.

The joys of being close to and sharing with others are about the togetherness force. This joy includes what we might call friendship; working with others on a project that is important to us all; the pleasure a parent finds in loving, nurturing, and protecting a child; romantic love; sensual and sexual pleasures; the enjoyment of great art or music (where we might experience an aesthetic connection with the artist or with what is portrayed); worship in a community we feel well connected with; or even just cheering in the stands along with a nameless crowd for the home team, "our" team.

What is included within the term *we*, a term that recognizes a sense of connection, and what is excluded in the opposite term, *they*, will vary from person to person and perhaps even from time to time. Some churches have a larger sense of "we" than others. They include more differences among members. Other churches draw very narrow and restricted lines and accept fewer differences.

There would be no human community and no human life without the togetherness force. Theologically, the togetherness force may be viewed as a part of, or an expression of, God in some way. Paul describes Christ in a number of his letters, saying "in him all things hold together" (Col. 1:17). The author of Hebrews speaks of God by saying "for whom and by whom all things consist" (Heb. 2:10). Christ is the very principle of unity in all things.

There can be a down side to the togetherness force in human community. Glue is sticky. In times of higher anxiety and in people with a lower level of emotional maturity, the glue gets stickier. The togetherness force tends to be experienced as a feeling that everyone in the group needs to think, feel, and behave in the same way, or that everyone *must* fulfill their roles in a particular, expected way.

As the level of chronic anxiety goes up and the level of emotional maturity goes down, a system has less tolerance for differences or deviations from what is expected. Emotional closeness is defined in those times as "sameness," being what one wants the other to be, or what the "authorities" want us to be.

Greater anxiety will increase the pressure for togetherness. And at lower levels of emotional maturity, this pressure will be experienced as "everyone must be the same" or fit in with some expectation for how everyone should be within particular roles; few or no exceptions are allowed.

In Germany in the 1930s, there was a very high level of anxiety. The primary source of this anxiety, but not the only one, related to the chaotic economic conditions. The Germans are an intelligent and well-educated people. But as their anxiety went up, they were increasingly attracted to the simplistic ideas of the Nazi party and Adolf Hitler, who offered, as the cause of Germany's problems, Jews, communists, homosexuals, and others whom he saw as social misfits who diluted the quality of what he called the "pure Aryan race."

In the midst of so much anxiety, the majority of the people lost their ability to think clearly, put aside their own deep spiritual beliefs and values, and participated in a social/political movement that helped them to feel better and more confident about themselves. They gave up many of their beliefs to go along with the "party line." Dictators thrive in situations where people are anxious, and so the Nazi party was voted into power.

Paradoxically, this kind of dictatorial pressure for unity leads automatically to greater fragmentation within groups. A certain percentage of people in the group experience the pressure as a threat to the self, and they then become reactive to this pressure. They perceive that there is less permission for them to be as they are, and feel overwhelmed with the demands of those pushing "unity" to give up who they are.

Even if Hitler had managed to win the war, his "empire" would have fallen apart from within, just as did the equally dictatorial communist bloc. The more any one group attempts to impose its will on another group, thus attempting to wipe out that group's sense of identity, the more pressure is being built for a rebellion. This will be true whether the pressure for sameness is coming from the conservative right or from the liberal left. It is the dynamic itself that creates this reality, not the politics of the group pushing for sameness.

The Individuality Force

Individuality is the biologically rooted life force that impels us to become our own persons, to become emotionally independent, distinct entities who think, feel, and act on the basis of what makes sense to us individually—who follow our own compass rather than the group compass. Individuality is what impels a child, for example, through the developmental process of growing up to go out and explore the world on his or her own and to become a person emotionally separate from the parents.

God has built into our biological and psychological makeup the normal developmental process of becoming an emotionally separate, individual self. We become able to think for ourselves; to have our own feelings, wishes, and intentions; and to act in ways that make sense to us. This is what the idea of individual responsibility is based on.

Nearly every inventor, great thinker, and explorer has had to go against the "group think" orientation of the particular field, in order to have his or her own thoughts and to put things together in new ways. Frequently the genius discoverer has been laughed at by his or her community and has had to endure their derision. It is the individuality force that allows us to explore new territory that no one else thinks is worthwhile or even possible.

We all thrive emotionally when we are able to be fully a self. We feel most alive and vital when we are able to pursue our dreams and goals. Giving up or losing our self to someone or something else leads to clinical depression.

The force for individuality might be expressed by those at lower levels of emotional maturity by being isolated, distant, and cut off from others, by avoiding contact with others, or by being the strong, silent, John Wayne type who moves through life with little sense of connection to others—the "rugged individualist."

Other immature aspects of individuality are the very self-centered or narcissistic behaviors designed to draw attention to the self or to get people in the environment focused on helping self or admiring self. These selfish expressions of individuality are essentially about the failure of a person to grow up emotionally. Biblical admonitions to "love others" make little impact on these immature people because they are not able to move from loving self to loving others.

True caring and love for others requires the mature development of the individuality force. The immature parent might either selfishly ignore a child's wants and needs under the influence of the individuality force or give the child whatever he or she wants under the influence of the togetherness force.

Maintaining a sense of self allows parents to stay connected with a child in difficult periods. A mature sense of individuality makes it easier to "hang in" with others during difficult and conflictual times without becoming reactive; it allows us to be in charge of self while connecting with others, rather than putting others in charge of us or demanding that others be what we want them to be.

The force for individuality must also be a part of God's nature, in that in God we see a strong sense of unique identity, as well as the ability to be extremely close to others. Jesus clearly portrays this in his life and ministry, rarely performing according to the expectations of the crowd or even of those close to him. He followed his own compass, rather than that of the leaders and popular beliefs of his day.

THE LIFE FORCES AND THE BIBLE

Clearly, God's love for and redemptive activity on behalf of the world is one expression of the togetherness force in God. God said "it is not good for man to be alone." Obviously it is "good" to be together with others. When Adam awoke from his "deep sleep," he expressed great joy in having one who was like him as a companion. But it is also clear, as every couple knows, that the man and woman have their differences from each other.

A part of being made in "the image of God" is about this relatedness to the "other." If anyone could say, "I have no need of others," it would be God, and yet the need for connection in God is where the biblical story begins. Connection is essential to the nature of God and to God's creation.

An essential part of connectedness, however, is individuality. Thus Jesus established his emotional separateness from his parents at an early age, as we see in the family's first trip to Jerusalem, when he left them to go teach in the temple at the age of twelve (Luke 2:41-51). In those days, twelve was the age a person was considered to have reached adulthood.

After his baptism by John, Jesus needed to go into the wilderness, alone, to be tested by Satan. No one else could do this for him or even with him. Each of us has our own wilderness experiences with which we must come to terms on our own, alone. They happen in a variety of ways, but it is in these experiences and in the process of temptation that we discover, just as Jesus had to do, our own solid beliefs, clarify our own commitments, and develop our sense of self and our unique mission in life.

Without his ability to develop into an individual, separate self, Jesus would not have been able to offer the unique perspective on God's relationship to the world that he did, nor would he have been able to fulfill God's mission for him. He was able to develop a sense of individuality *and* to maintain a sense of continuity and connection with the history and tradition of Judaism. Emotional separateness did not mean he threw all that history over and disconnected himself from it; thus, we see the power of the togetherness force. But his separateness did mean he was able to bring a new perspective, a new interpretation, and a new message about God's love for and redemptive activity in the world—within that history and tradition.

In 1 Corinthians 9–13, we can see Paul attempting to deal with the factions present in that church by balancing these two life forces. On the one hand, he is calling for unity within the Corinthian church, the body of Christ, which did have significant divisions within it, asking them to "have the mind of Christ" and to be "imitators" of him (Paul), as he is an imitator of Christ.

And on the other hand, he calls the Corinthians to respect a broad diversity of Christian beliefs, behaviors, and practices. He says one part of the body cannot impose conformity and sameness on another part; if all parts of the body were a hand or foot or eye, the body would stop being functional. Having "the mind of Christ" must include respecting the broad diversity present within his body.

No one way is the best way, except, as Paul says in chapter 13, the "more excellent way" of love. The way of love, in fact, requires a strong sense of individuality and is quite comfortable with diversity. The way of love is a way of maintaining both the unique sense of everyone's individuality and mature togetherness.

In addition to the Gospels and Paul's letters, the Book of Acts gives us many examples of this tension between individuality and togetherness in the early church. Peter first had to take a stand that the church (which consisted only of Jews, of course) should include Gentiles within its fellowship. But he did not go far enough even with this position, and together he and the other church leaders began to say that, essentially, Gentiles should first become Jews before they could truly be in the church. Paul then had to stand against them all, face to face in a dramatic encounter, with practically no support at first, to say that God had really done a new thing in Jesus and created a new avenue of access to God and salvation. Eventually the early church agreed with Paul, but the community achieved this new understanding only because Paul was willing to stand, alone, by his understanding of the gospel.

And theologically, even within the doctrine of the Trinity, which emphasizes the unity of the three persons of the Godhead, there is also an emphasis on the separateness of each person. We affirm in that doctrine that each person in the Godhead is fully separate and fully an individual "person," as well as fully God. And for us to be united or at one with God must function in the same way. It does not mean the obliteration of the individual personality or the fusion of one person into the other.

THE LIFE FORCES IN THE CHURCH

During times of higher anxiety, the less mature people in the church seek to promote sameness and conformity as the way to achieve unity or togetherness in the community. To use Paul's image, this would be like saying we must all be a foot or a hand or an eye.

This church will have a strong "other" focus: It will be watching to see if others are conforming to expectations about how they "should" be and to what extent they are being what is considered by the leadership "truly Christian." The element of judging the faith and behavior of others will be prominent. This was a primary factor affecting the emotional atmosphere of relationships at Valley View. Each person was clear that others were not being the way they "should" be.

More mature individuals, who have a stronger sense of their own self or their individuality, experience mature togetherness as attraction to, interest in, and curiosity about others, especially about getting to know others' differences. In this form of unity, there is greater comfort with diversity, variety, and uniqueness.

Mature individuality inclines us to work at defining more clearly our own beliefs and life principles and thinking about our own behaviors, to see if we are conforming to what we say we believe. It involves a "self focus" rather than a judgmental "other focus." We pay more attention to our own problems and difficulties and take responsibility for ourselves. In the words of Jesus, these church members focus less on the "speck of sawdust" in the eye of others and deal more with the "beam of wood" in their own.

At Third Church, even though no one welcomed the task of dealing with the uncomfortable mess on that Sunday morning, everyone was able to modify personal wishes and plans for the morning in order to accommodate the larger need, dealing with the tasks at hand. Members demonstrated a flexibility that allowed them to deal with the unique challenges of the morning and, more or less, to proceed with their regular duties at the same time. And they demonstrated a respect for each other's particular needs, or mistakes, without labeling the other "wrong" or "bad" or somehow "inadequate." As a result, the church members were able to work cooperatively to get the job done in a relatively smooth way.

At Valley View, however, where the sense of mutual respect was very weak and the strong sense that others were somehow "wrong" was strong, thus producing a high level of threat and reactivity, the church had a much more difficult road to travel to get the job done. Members responded with less flexibility to the requirements of the situation. Each new problem, each communication between participants, each move on one person's part to get some comfort for self when dealing with the problems implied a lack of respect for the other, to which the other reacted in kind.

In times of crisis, as people with lower emotional maturity become more anxious, there is a tendency for the togetherness force to be strongly activated and for people to insist that all others operate out of the same position or set of beliefs. But this automatic, unthinking position will usually end up being destructive to the community. In a crisis, unity in action, if it is to be achieved at all, will happen as a result of people's ability (and freedom) to think things through for themselves, based on all the available facts, and then respectfully to share their understandings with one another.

QUESTIONS

For Your Own Thinking

1. How comfortable are you with the differences within your congregation? How, or in what ways, have you demonstrated this comfort?

2. Who are you most different from in your church, and how do you deal with this difference?

3. What could you learn or have you learned from this difference?

4. Think of some times and relationships in which you have managed to stay well connected with those with whom you also differed? How did you manage to do this?

5. At one point Jesus was quoted as saying, "[Whoever] is not with me is against me" (Matt. 12:30). At another time, however, he said, "[Whoever] is not against us is for us" (Mark 9:40). Which statement do you lean toward in your own personal life? How do you manage to find a balance?

6. To what extent do you get focused on how others act toward you, as opposed to how you act toward others?

For Group Discussion

1. What specific differences does your congregation seem to deal well with? Which ones cause more problems?

2. How do members of your congregation attempt to achieve "peace and unity" in the church, in the midst of significant differences?

3. To what extent is "unity" defined as "sameness" and "lack of diversity" in your church? Give examples.

4. How much "sameness" is needed in a congregation in order to feel "unified"? Is there such a thing as "too much diversity"?

5. How does your church draw boundaries and decide who belongs to "us" and who belongs to "them"?

6. If having "the mind of Christ" includes respecting the diversity of members of the body, how well does your congregation do this?

7. What other biblical passages or theological themes seem relevant to your thinking about peace, unity, and diversity in the church?

5

CLOSENESS, DISTANCE, AND THE CONGREGATION

Therefore a man leaves his father and his mother and cleaves to his wife.   *(Genesis 2:24)*

And he came and preached peace to you who were far off and peace to those who were near.   *(Ephesians 2:17)*

THE CLOSE/DISTANT DYNAMIC

Michael Kerr, a colleague of Murray Bowen, tells the story of a group of porcupines enduring a particularly cold winter. In spite of being natural loners, they discovered that when they moved closer together, they felt more comfortable because they could share their bodily warmth with one another. If they moved too close, however, they were pricked by each other's needles. Through trial and error they were able to establish a distance that allowed them some benefit of each other's warmth, without being jabbed by each other's needles. They called this distance from one another "right and proper."

A major factor affecting the sense of community in a church is the relative level of emotional closeness and distance members have with one another that they regard as "right and proper." To a visitor, one church will feel "cold," and the members will seem "too distant" from one another (or at least from the visitor). In another church, the person will feel "jabbed" by members who seem to impinge on one another, from the visitor's point of view.

Just as cultures vary in what is considered the correct physical distance people should stand from one another during their social contacts, churches can vary by the amount of emotional closeness and distance that members have with one another. This closeness/distance factor reflects the way individuals and groups manage themselves within the life forces of togetherness and individuality.

ABANDONMENT AND ENGULFMENT

Growing up and becoming mature is a matter of developing greater comfort with becoming physically and emotionally separate people. Physical separation is easy to accomplish, but emotional separation is much more difficult to achieve. Most people arrive at adulthood with what Bowen would call a certain amount of "unresolved emotional attachment" to their parents and other family members. Many of us go through our whole lives with these attachments unresolved.

Each shift in the close/distant continuum within a family or a congregation presents an emotional challenge to members of the system. Individuals vary in the amount of emotional closeness with and distance from others that they find comfortable. The level of comfort could be called the person's comfort zone.

If we create a continuum from closeness to distance, then person A might have a comfort zone that looks like this:

Zones of Comfort

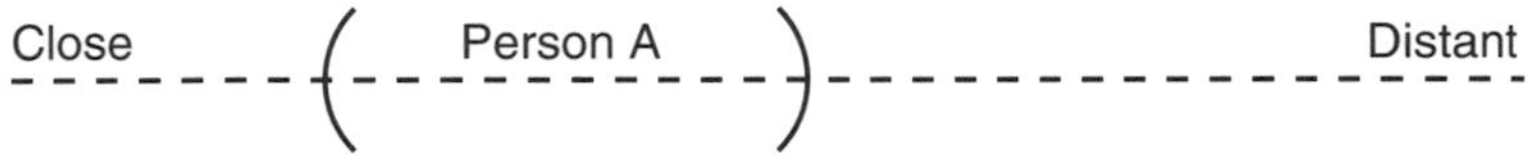

FIGURE 6

However, person B's comfort zone might look like this:

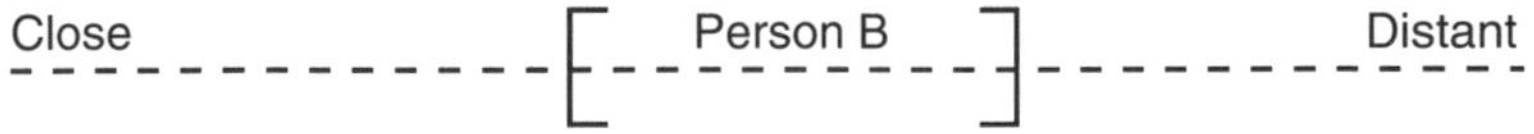

FIGURE 7

A relationship between A and B would look like this, with five areas or zones of emotional comfort:

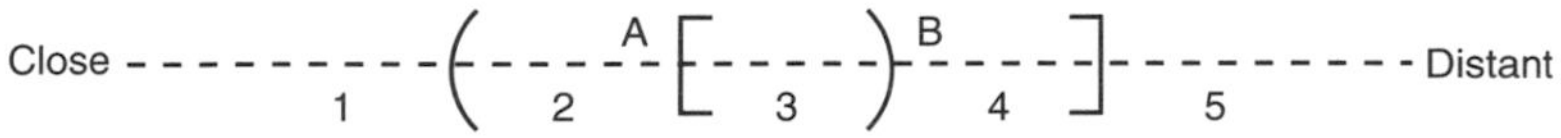

FIGURE 8

Zone 1 represents a level of emotional closeness that neither A nor B would feel comfortable with; both would consider it too close. Zone 2 represents the area that A wishes B would enjoy with him and tries to encourage B to come into, but B would still find the zone, for the most part, too close. Zone 3 is their mutual or shared comfort zone, where their two comfort zones overlap. When they are operating in this area together, they both feel comfortable. Zone 4 is the area of greater emotional distance that B wishes A would maintain, so that she would feel less "jabbed" by him. However this area feels too distant for A. Zone 5 is the area of emotional distance that neither person would be comfortable with; it would feel too distant to them both.

Zones 2 and 4 tend to be the areas in which people can feel either abandoned or engulfed by others. When A is relatively calm, he might experience B's distance as "no big deal" and get on with his life. But if A were feeling anxiously needy of greater closeness with B and B did not respond, A could feel emotionally abandoned by B.

So with a higher level of anxiety, A might feel desperately needy of B, and B's distance would be a big problem. In fact, the distance itself could become the threat, or at least exacerbate A's anxiety. If B maintained her distance, in spite of A's efforts to bring her close emotionally, A might become either increasingly fearful or angry, but both feelings in A would be stimulated by his sense of being abandoned.

As for B, there would be times when she could quite comfortably involve herself in A's concerns and not feel uncomfortable with this. She could at these times "give of her self" willingly and experience no loss of her self. If B were feeling particularly comfortable, she might even be able to stretch into zone 2 for a period of time and satisfy some of A's neediness. A would feel reassured by this. While B may not feel fully comfortable, A would find B very caring and would feel particularly close to her.

But at other times B could begin to feel "engulfed" by A's problems or by his life and to feel like she was losing her own identity or her own sense of having a separate life. At these times, B definitely will not move into zone 2, and in fact will encourage A to be more like her and to operate at the greater distance of zone 4. She may say that she is beginning to feel smothered by A and his neediness.

At the most extreme level, B will begin to feel totally overwhelmed by A and his life or problems. More and more often, she will wish to pull back, saying she needs some space, some room to breath, or some time alone. She may fantasize about living alone, threaten to leave him, or actually leave.

Churches often try to maintain what they think of as the "right and proper" distance between members. However, it is difficult to maintain a particular level of closeness and distance in any congregation's life because some winters are colder than others. When they feel too cold, some individuals will try to move closer to others, who may feel jabbed by these moves for closeness and then reactively distance themselves from those trying to be closer.

Members in a congregation are quite attuned to one another's emotional movement on the continuum. Members can frequently read even slight shifts in another person's direction of movement (towards or away from self) or the other's level of comfort. It's as if we always have our finger on the tautness of the rubber band between us and can sense what is happening to the level of tension in the band.

For example, someone might normally feel quite close to her pastor or to a friend in the congregation. The two operate mostly within each other's comfort zone. But then, during a stressful time, the pastor or friend becomes more withdrawn and less available to her. She might begin to think this greater distance is about her (rather than about the pastor's or friend's way of dealing with stress) and become upset with this distance. She could then begin anxiously to pursue the other to try to reduce the perceived distance between them, so that she could feel calmer.

PURSUERS AND DISTANCERS

When the sense of equilibrium in the mobile is lost and the system seems out of balance, and when we become anxious about this, we use the mechanisms of emotional pursuit and distance as one way to rebalance the system. When it appears to us that our upset is "caused" by someone important to us moving away from us, we often pursue them, trying to bring them back into a closer relationship. When it appears to us that our upset is "caused" by someone trying to be closer to us than we feel comfortable with, we then distance from them.

In the weeks and months that followed her resignation, Maureen Niven's distancing from the church stimulated anxiety in those who had been closer to her; they felt abandoned. Some of these people pursued her by almost begging her not to leave. Others blamed Roy, the pastor, for being so hard on her and said he should try to get her back. Roy in fact was relieved because he had not liked having Maureen in the "closeness" of that position.

In another church, a pastor, suddenly and unexpectedly, lost his wife in a car accident. At the same time, his daughter had been close to the stage of leaving home. While before his wife's death he had been ready for and looking forward to this transition, within months after his wife's death he went out and bought a new large house, with a pool, and stocked it full of all kinds of grownup toys for him and his "child" to play with.

He now wanted to keep his adult child as close to home as possible. The two of them began to fight with each other, which they had never done before. In counselling, they began to identify and talk about these issues for the first time openly. The daughter said that she had stayed at home longer than she had intended to because she knew dad was anxious about being alone. She knew the new house was an effort to keep her close. She was feeling guilty about wanting to leave, and frustrated and angry that she didn't think she could leave him. She also resented his pursuit of her.

At the same time, the pastor was increasingly neglecting his pastoral duties. This had an impact on the life of the church, and it initiated a rocky period in the congregation's relationship with the pastor until what had happened could be sorted out. In an attempt to deal with the change, the church leadership pursued him angrily, and at first, until he understood better what was happening, he kept his distance from them and from what he regarded as their "unreasonable demands." The shift within his family life and the anxiety in the family system associated with this translated into anxiety in the church system and affected the general level of anxiety there.

Pursuing and distancing are not inborn personality characteristics. They depend on the situation and the particular relationship. One younger woman's husband died relatively early in their marriage. While very much in love with him, her one complaint about him was that he was not very emotionally open with her and would not talk about feelings with her the way she wanted. She continually pursued him emotionally, while he distanced. After his death, when she eventually began to think about dating again, she intentionally set out to look for a man who was more emotionally sensitive, open, and able to talk about feelings. She found such a man, was thrilled, and married him. After the first year of marriage, her complaint was that he always wanted to talk about feelings and, especially, what was going on inside of her. She became the emotional distancer in this relationship and began to behave with him more like her first husband had with her. She said she now understood what it had been like for him.

So inside of every pursuer is a distancer, and vice versa. Which role a person plays depends on the situation and who is taking responsibility for which part of the close/distant functioning at a particular time. The parties may need similar levels of distance and closeness, but they may manage this by each person being responsible for only one function: one partner, for the closeness; and the other, for the distance. In most workable relationships, the parties can be somewhat flexible and take responsibility for either side. They don't get stuck in a single role, with one always doing the pursuing and the other of always being responsible for the distance.

A very common emotional pattern in relationships looks like this. When both A and B are calm, they may operate comfortably within each other's comfort zone. But an element they experience as stressful is added. If they have different ways of coping with stress (with one needing to talk with someone in order to figure out what to do, and the other needing some time alone to figure out what to do or to let things cool down), then they will typically begin to move differently on the close/distant continuum. This is stage 1 in a common emotional process.

In addition to the original stress experience itself, the movement pattern of each begins to exacerbate the experience of stress for the other. As both people become more anxious, they intensify their patterns of movement, pursuing and distancing, increasing the anxiety between the two even more, with one becoming fearful of abandonment and the other fearful of engulfment. This intensification is stage 2 in the process.

Distancers can always outdistance pursuers. At some point the pursuer decides this is the case; she gives up and does what is called reactive distancing. Within a short period of time, the former distancer begins to sense that the pursuer is no longer pursuing or taking responsibility for the closeness. At that point the former distancer will begin to feel the distance between them (rather than too much closeness) and become the pursuer, trying to achieve some level of connection. This is stage 3.

If the former pursuer then responds to this pursuit by the former distancer, there may be a time of comfortable connection between them. But soon the old pattern of pursuer and distancer will be reinstated, as new anxiety is introduced, and they will be stuck again in their old roles, recyclying the same emotional process. This is stage 4.

After too many cycles of this kind, the person who becomes the reactive distancer will no longer respond to the pursuit from the former distancer. She will put up a wall, saying things like "Where were you when I needed you? I can't count on this desire for closeness being real. It's too little too late. I don't care or feel anything for you anymore." She maintains her distance and this is stage 5.

In particularly intense and bitter relationships, at this point they will both establish a fixed distance between them and perhaps become life-long enemies, lobbing little bombs of criticism at each other over their walls of self-protection. This becomes stage 6, the final bitter step in the process of emotional divorce.

Perhaps you have seen this pattern develop between two people or two groups in the church. Probably you have experienced milder and less intense forms of this pattern yourself. Nearly all of us have participated in stages 1 to 4, and perhaps even stage 5, with one or two important people in our lives. Stage 6 is less common but it is typical of very bitter divorces. The legal divorce does not end the emotional intensity of the relationship and the couple can keep fighting with each other for another twenty years. Intense friendships have occasionally ended in this kind of stand-off, and congregations and their former pastors sometimes reach this last stage.

CLOSENESS/DISTANCE AND THE BIBLE

The Bible is full of stories of comings and goings, of connecting and separating; it is a book of active verbs. It tells lively stories about people on the move. Ours is a dynamic God of action, as well as a God of contemplation. And God's people are expected to be active, as well as thoughtful. This action includes movement toward and away from other people. One could study the Bible simply to observe patterns of movement that increase or decrease closeness and distance: who connects with whom and separates from whom.

One of the elements that made belonging to the early church such a dynamic experience is the variety of types and classes of people who were brought together in it: men and women; intellectuals and laborers; wealthy slave owners and their slaves; Gentiles and Jews; people of little religious experience and highly religious people; and people of various racial and ethnic backgrounds.

Churches today have become much more homogeneous in their makeup than the early church was. Social elements like class, race, and culture tend to determine who we will include in our fellowship, and who we will not include; who we are close to, and who we are not.

Church systems can keep themselves stagnant by building locked-in close/distant arrangements that allow them to connect only with similar kinds of people. An alive, spirit-filled, well-functioning church, just like a mobile, allows people, like different parts of the mobile, to move closer together at one point and further apart at another.

Stuck churches are sometimes referred to as being full of "cliques." The reason any of us are tempted to "cliquishness" is that belonging to a clique helps us to feel safe and comfortable; this is what sameness offers us. Meeting new people or becoming related in new ways can provoke anxiety for many of us. Closed emotional systems present us with fewer challenges.

As Christians, we believe that life comes to us from outside ourselves, that God's Holy Spirit continues to bring us new life and energy every day ("give us this day our daily bread" is both a spiritual and a material request). When we operate within a closed system, it is more difficult for the Spirit of God to feed and nurture us with newness of life.

Look at the many biblical stories about God bringing something new into people's lives. Notice how often the people try to avoid God's new thing, to keep their distance, or at least to wrestle with it while trying to come to terms with it. In the process of this anxious growth, all of us become energized and receive new life. But some part of each one of us can still identify with the Israelites, who complained to Moses about leading them out of slavery in Egypt. At least in Egypt, in bondage as slaves, the Israelites knew what they could count on every day; in spite of the hardships and sufferings, there was a comfortable routine to it all.

Paul spoke of those who were "near" to God and those who were "far off" (Eph. 2:17), meaning Jews and Gentiles. Paul was saying that because of God's action in Christ, all people have an equal standing before God and have equal access to salvation through God's grace. In Christ, God has made peace with and reconciled both those near and those far off.

In Luke 6:32-36, the author addresses the Christians in the church for whom he wrote this Gospel, reporting Jesus as saying (in my very free translation of his words) "it is no great accomplishment to love those who are like us [close], this is after all just a kind of loving ourselves. The bigger challenge, and the gospel call, is to love those who are different from us [distant], those who do not share the same assumptions about life that we do." Jesus directly challenges here the idea that closeness, or love, is based on sameness.

In the words of Peter's vision (Acts 10:15), we have no right to call unclean [and to therefore keep our distance from] that which God has called clean. The differences that exist are real, but they cannot be a basis for our refusal to have communion with, or be close to, others.

CLOSENESS/DISTANCE AND CHURCH LEADERSHIP

These close/distant relationships in a church—both relationships between members and the relationship of the community to the denomination and the larger world—are a key category for observing and understanding human community and for bringing about change in that community.

The leaders of a church have a great deal to say, primarily through their example, about patterns of movement within a congregation or in relation to the world. The more mature and secure the leaders, the more freely and flexibly they can follow God into new areas of connecting and service. Here are just a few thoughts about how the close/distant dynamic affects church life.

1. The evangelistic ministry of the church is one area that could be affected by increased flexibility in this pattern of movement. A fair percentage of people keep their distance from the church and do not become involved because they believe they would have to become something they are not in order to be "acceptable" to the church community. They see church as a place where they will be perceived as too different and told what to believe and how to behave. They believe they won't be accepted just for who and what they are.

2. Our fellowship with one another within the church is affected by this close/distant dynamic. We ourselves keep a distance from certain other people within the church and do not become close to one another. We often just don't allow ourselves to be known even at very basic levels, let alone in more emotionally intimate ways.

At Valley View, Maureen Niven had never figured out a way to adequately represent her beliefs to the pastor about the church school curriculum. Whenever she tried to discuss it with him, he immediately came on strong with what she called the official party line. She then thought it was really not okay to say what she thought, and she just kept quiet. She kept her distance, emotionally, not openly sharing her own experience and thoughts, as a way to try to preserve her sense of self. Roy kept his distance from her because he was not interested in her experience and views.

People need to feel safe enough to allow themselves to feel close to others or to allow themselves to go their own way. Dealing with the underlying anxieties related to these forces is the major source of growth for us all. Leadership needs to be sensitive to the issue of safety between members of the congregation and the congregation's movement in the world. Safety allows a flexibility of movement, whereas anxiety constricts us and makes us cautious.

3. Remember also that this dynamic involves not only church members in relationship to each other but also each member's various other emotional systems. Some of the most active laypeople in the church might actually be using the church and their jobs as leaders to distance themselves from situations in their families, work, or friendships. This is a part of what was going on with Marie Fontana at Valley View, and with Roy in response to her. Her own high level of activity in the church and their apparent closeness with each other was based on having distance from their spouses. This is not a healthy thing for the people involved, the church, or their marriages and families, no matter how hard these people work on the church's behalf.

4. When leadership is motivated by a fear of abandonment, two quite different styles of interaction may develop that, on the surface, look totally opposite. One style, which is not often recognized as emotional pursuit, is to take charge of the relationship, to be dictatorial, or at least highly directive. These people believe that if they allow another person to behave in a way that makes sense to that person, then he or she won't stay connected; so they take charge of the relationship in an authoritarian way. Marital partners do this with one another.

The ones in charge of the relationship look more independent, but they are really very dependent on the support of the apparently dependent ones; they need the "dependent ones" to agree to conform to their wishes. If those who appear more dependent were to become stronger and do their own thinking and decision making, then, after an intense period of trying to "whip" them back into their old roles, the independent-looking leader would melt and actually become quite dependent.

The other style is just the converse. It involves behavior in which a person is willing, compliantly, to give up a great deal of self in order to maintain a closeness or to feel accepted. The greatest fear or source of anxiety for such people is that they couldn't get along on their own, that they need the connection with the other to be okay themselves. The anxiety we feel about the possibility of abandonment or loss of self through lack of connection to important others, is one of the most powerful motivating forces we can experience.

5. There is nothing inherently wrong with pursuing others for connection. There would be no relationships without someone taking responsibility for connecting with others. There would be no church if we did not pursue others and seek to relate to them. The togetherness force inspires us to move toward others, and inspires others to respond.

But a rule of thumb church leaders need to be particularly aware of is; Never pursue those who repeatedly distance from you. If you do, then you will get into the pursuit/distance cycle, and it will be frustrating for all concerned.

In relationships that work well, both parties need to take some responsibility for the connection, and both must respect the need for distance when it is sought by one side. These principles have a great deal to do with successful boards and committees, as well as friendships and other close relationships.

6. A frequent way we pursue others is to try to inspire guilt in them, or to make them feel obligated to do what we think they "should" do. While outwardly a certain percentage of people will comply with our expectations and more or less do what we think they should, inwardly they will begin to distance from us, and eventually, if this pattern continues, they will disappear from the congregation.

Feelings of guilt usually inspire emotional, if not physical, distance. Obviously there are legitimate experiences of guilt based on a person's actual transgressions. But a good case can be made that it is not the guilt that "makes" us repent and move back toward the one we have offended. Other elements may be involved in this movement, not the least of which is a hope for reconciliation and reconnection.

People have to believe they can comfortably say no to requests made of them before they will comfortably say yes and then actually do what they agree to do. Often, those who think they cannot say no comfortably, because they would feel guilty, say yes to our requests for their help, but then they fail to do the job they were asked to do, or fail to do it adequately. If we, as leaders, make it hard for people to say no, then we are setting ourselves up for frustration, as well as losing a potentially important connection with others.

7. It would seem then that a major quality of mature leadership is to feel comfortable with others' distance from us and not to become anxious about their "abandoning" us or abandoning our view of their responsibilities. This is well illustrated in Luke's story of the prodigal son. Helmut Thieliecke, the German pastor and theologian, called this story the parable of the waiting father. The father clearly loved his son and was sorry to see him take all of his inheritance and go waste it in the "far country." But he did not anxiously pursue his son, knowing that this pursuit could well drive his son farther away. After a period of time, the son "came to himself" and realized that his distancing from his father had been to his own detriment and that he would go back to his father, even if it meant becoming a servant in his father's house. He became responsible for reconnecting with his father.

8. Another way we can pursue others is through our preaching and teaching in the church. Some sermons, especially the evangelistic ones and those that call others to social action, can be particularly pursuing. These can still be done in a way that respects others and allows them to decide whether they will respond to the call or the invitation.

We can best teach others when they are moving toward us. All efforts to "teach" those who are moving down the road away from us will only intensify the distance. If the father had chased his son down the road, saying "You'll be sorry for this! You will come back on your knees!" there is a good chance the son would never have come back, no matter how intensely unhappy he was.

When people are moving away from us, it is important to listen to them, rather than try to teach them. They may have information for us to hear, but they will also feel more important and more understood—to the extent that we do our best to understand. Listening is an important form of maintaining a connection, and it is the best we can do when people are keeping their distance.

9. Wise leadership knows when to invite connection, when to lis-

ten rather than to speak, and when to be comfortable with distance. There are times when it is appropriate to pursue. In those times, pursuit demonstrates our caring for others, our interest in them, and their importance to us. But at other times, nonanxious waiting and listening communicate caring and respect. The more mature the church leadership, the more wisdom they will have about knowing when to move toward others and when to wait as they move away; neither action will create anxiety in the mature leaders.

QUESTIONS

For Your Own Thinking

1. Have you noticed any variation in your willingness to be close to or your desire to be distant from other members of the congregation over the years of your membership? What seems to affect this? Is it affected by events in your own life, for example, your family, work situation, social life, and so forth?

2. How comfortable are you with your present level of connection with others in your church?

3. To what extent do you think you might experience abandonment and engulfment in relation to your church?

4. Are there particular people you want to be closer to or more distant from in the church? How is this affecting your level of comfort in the church?

5. Generally, do you find yourself more often in the role of distancer or pursuer? When, how, and with whom does this role vary?

6. How sensitive are you to other people's emotional comfort zones? How flexible can you be, relating to them from a position of either greater closeness or distance? What does this say about you?

For Group Discussion

1. How well does your congregation seem to be able to negotiate the "right and proper" distance between members?

2. How well do the leaders negotiate distances with each other and with members of the congregation?

3. Where and in what ways do you sense anxiety in the congregation around closeness and distance?

4. Using the graph of the five zones of comfort on page 67, try to identify whether some of the "hot" issues in the congregation are

actually about closeness/distance, rather than simply about the issues as such? If people felt more comfortable emotionally, would the identified issue be as hot? If the "self" of members felt safer and less threatened, would the level of reactivity around the issue be as high?

5. Take one hot issue in the church. How is the sense of self, or the identity of members, and their sense of connection with one another affected by this issue?

6. In what ways do leaders and members of this church pursue and distance from one another?

7. To what extent is your congregation caught in comfortable cliquishness, rather than allowing the new and different to enter in? How are you as leaders dealing with this?

8. What needs to happen around the close/distant dynamic in your church?

9. What other biblical and theological themes come to mind around this theme of closeness and distance in the church?

6

FOOLISHNESS AND WISDOM
IN CHURCH LEADERSHIP

For wisdom is better than jewels, and all that you may desire cannot compare with her.　　　　　　　　　　　　　　*(Proverbs 8:11)*

And [Jesus] grew and became strong, filled with wisdom; and the favor of God was upon him.　　　　　　　　　　　　*(Luke 2:40)*

THE BASIC INGREDIENTS OF FOOLISHNESS AND WISDOM: FUSION AND DIFFERENTIATION

Both congregations in chapter 1 faced the same situation: a cold church building and backed-up sewers. Each experienced a certain amount of anxiety about the situation, and they were both under the influence of the togetherness and individuality forces. But Valley View ended up with a significant amount of distance and conflict between its members, and Third Church pulled together, working more closely and cooperatively to deal with the challenge.

In any group, the level of stability, the amount of cohesiveness and cooperation, and the ability to accomplish its mission, is dependent on the average level of emotional maturity in the group. This chapter will begin to explore what "emotional maturity" means and its implications for church leadership. In biblical language, emotional maturity is best described by the word *wisdom*.

In family systems theory, fusion and differentiation are the emotional processes that lead, respectively, to less or more emotional maturity. These two terms refer to the way we manage the two life forces of individuality and togetherness within ourselves and in our relations with others. They are about the degree of emotional merging and emotional separateness in our relationships with one another.

One is never fully "fused" or "differentiated," as if these were total states of being, but one is always "more or less fused" or "more or less differentiated." While the two churches looked qualitatively different, in fact their differences can best be described quantitatively, that is, as two different points on this continuum.

Fusion and differentiation are not the same as togetherness and individuality, nor are they the same as emotional closeness and distance. Fusion and differentiation are about emotional process in relationships. The word *process* refers to how we manage something. Fusion and differentiation refer to two processes in particular:

1. internally, the degree to which a person can separate thinking and feeling, and bring greater objectivity to his or her own inevitably subjective stance; and

2. interpersonally, the degree to which a person can be clear or more objective about the emotional separateness between self and other, knowing what is self and self's responsibility, and what is not.

The emotional maturity of differentiation allows us to think things through for ourselves and to be able to act more effectively in relation to others in the congregational system. This clarity and maturity becomes more difficult to achieve as the level of anxiety goes up in a group.

FUSION AND FOOLISHNESS

The eighteenth-century novelist Lawrence Stern once wrote, "Some people carry their hearts in their heads; very many carry their heads in their hearts. The difficulty is to keep them apart and get both actively working together." This pretty well states what family systems theory means by attempting to keep thinking and feeling separate. It is not a matter of one being better than the other; both are needed in life. But it helps to know the difference between the two and when to act more out of one or the other.

All of the people at Valley View had difficulty separating their thoughts from their feelings; they automatically reacted to their personal sense of threat (feeling), rather than being more reflective. Their subjective feelings and their limited, more defensive perceptions of the situation contaminated their ability to be more objective and reduced their ability to think things through more clearly and to make better decisions.

Their experience of the situation and of the reactions of others within the relationship process were pretty self-centered. Each one took the events of the morning as somehow being about them or reflecting on them. They could only feel how they personally were affected by the situation. They were not able to develop a wider angle picture or a more objective perception of the situation that removed them from the center of the picture.

Each person behaved in ways designed to try to reduce his or her own personal level of threat and anxiety, with the typical flight/fight strategies a person employs when the sense of threat is high. When faced with the acute anxiety of the difficult Sunday morning circumstances they faced, their normally high sense of chronic anxiety, or feeling-based reactions, took over and ran them.

Also, fusion confuses both persons and responsibility; a lack of clarity about what is "me" and what is "not me." At Valley View, each person had the sense that someone else was making him or her feel and behave as he or she did; each person believed he or she did something because of what someone else did. They thought, if only so-and-so would change, then I could behave differently. They lost their own sense of emotional separateness, or autonomy, and their sense of responsibility for self. Each one denied his or her own responsibility in the situation as it developed, blamed others for failing to be more responsible, and avoided looking at his or her own role in the emotional difficulties of the morning.

If confronted about his or her behavior, each might say something like, "I wouldn't be this way (for example, angry), if you weren't the way you are. You make me behave this way." They would sound like the classic situation involving a wife of an alcoholic complaining to her husband about his drinking: he says, "I wouldn't drink so much if you didn't nag me so much"; to which she replies, "I wouldn't nag you so much if you didn't drink so much." Each person sees the other person as responsible for, or causing, his or her own behavior. Each person's explanation is some version of the excuse that comedian Flip Wilson's character, Geraldine, offers: "The devil made me do it!" When we are more fused, it is hard to know who is in charge of whom and who is responsible for what.

There is no church or group or individual that operates without a certain amount of fusion, and most of us are more, rather than less, fused. While fusion is not the same as sinfulness, it is just as prevalent and presents some interesting parallels in its functioning. When talking with God in the Garden of Eden, for example, Adam experienced threat in God's question to him and tried to blame both the woman and God ("the woman *whom thou gavest* to be with me") for his eating of the forbidden tree. He denies responsibility for his action and tries to place it elsewhere, which is one aspect of fusion.

Almost the first words the custodian Larry Lambert at Valley View said to Stu McGuire over the phone were, "Mister . . . *you* got a big mess on your hands here," avoiding any responsibility for dealing with the situation. This is a lot different from the way Wayne Higby posed the situation to Andy White at Third Church. Wayne calmly and factually stated the condition of things at the church and demonstrated a willingness to think with Andy about how to approach the situation, including what his own role would be.

Andy's first reaction to the news was a personal one, focused on how this situation impacted him, but he quickly got over this reaction and began to work at getting a bigger picture and thinking issues through clearly. He was then able to work with Wayne to think about what needed to be done by whom, in what order, so they were able to begin to deal with the situation. They didn't get stuck on dealing with their level of threat, or focus on blame, or go into attack/defend mode. They were able to just get on with the job at hand, cooperatively.

Back at Valley View, a little later in the story, Larry accuses Stu of having no concern for his safety ("Are you trying to get me blown up?") or comfort (he didn't want to have to shovel snow and ice if the church was cold and there was no place to get warm). He defends against being implicated in the problems by going on the attack.

Stu then begins a similar process of blaming other people for his morning being disturbed, asserting that Larry refuses to do his job properly. Stu says he is stuck with Larry because of the pastor who hired him. The sewer backups are Larry's fault, and so forth. Later, when Stu tries to lay all of this at the pastor's feet, Roy then blames Stu and others for their lack of responsibility, and Stu and Lolly then blame it all not only on the pastor but also on the denominational leadership, whom they see as responsible for what they regard as the generally poor quality of pastors today.

Some of Lolly's friends aren't sure whether to include the pastor's wife in the problems or not. Janet Whalley, the day-care director, blames the situation on the pastor and the congregation and their lack of concern for neighborhood ministry. And Maureen Niven blames her problems in the church school that Sunday morning on the pastor and the denomination. And so the morning continues in much the same vein, each blaming others and leaving self and self's role in the difficulties out of the picture.

Each person attempted to get more comfort for self by shifting responsibility elsewhere. Under the influence of the fusion process, we do what we can, usually impulsively, to relieve the discomfort, even if the solution is a short-sighted one. In fusion, we have less ability to tolerate anxiety and to resist being governed by it.

The lack of emotional separateness, or the fusion between the leaders at Valley View, made them both prone to be critical of one another and exquisitely sensitive to criticism. Their contact was "prickly." They were easily triggered to react emotionally to one another, which made it difficult for them to work together. They all felt unappreciated and uncared for and could not give what they each deeply yearned for: a sense of approval, love, and acceptance.

When two magnets are brought within each other's force field, they immediately orient themselves to each other. They can no longer exist autonomously. They don't even have a choice about it; it is an automatic occurrence. There was something of the same magnetic quality to the interactions that morning at Valley View. The more emotionally interdependent people are, the more easily threatened they are by the differences of others. After the fact, Roy was a little surprised by how he had spoken to Stu, but he had felt like he had no control over the words, that they just poured out. Similarly, his warm response to Marie's "understanding" what things were like for him and his being drawn to her also came automatically, as did his colder hostility to his apparently not understanding wife, Joy. So whether the reaction is one of being angry or being warm ("You made me love you, I didn't want to do it"), in fusion we see the other as being in charge of our reactions.

As fusion increases within a congregation, members increasingly confuse feelings and fact. What various members "feel" is taken for what is factually the case. If one feels rejected, then it is assumed one is actually rejected. If one feels threatened, then it is assumed that there is someone actually being threatening. The subjective feeling world is more dominant in fused congregations.

If a pastor feels betrayed by a committee chair who thinks differently about a church program than he or she does and cuts off emotionally from that chair, then both the pastor and the congregation lose. Again, the ability to develop an emotional environment in which even deeply held differences can be contained will be a boon not only to the pastor and committee chair but to the whole congregation.

People at Valley View could not maintain a sense of objectivity in the midst of their differences; they were run by their subjectivity. It felt good to Roy to sound off angrily to Andy and Janet and to the congregation in his sermon, but the short-term good feelings were not going to be worth the headache and difficulties those moments helped to create in the long term. Feeling-based reactions, while they may "feel good" when trying to relieve our own uneasiness in difficult relationships, can be unhelpful guides to behavior.

This is not to oppose having or expressing feelings, as such. Feelings are important barometers of what is going on with us in any particular situation. It is better to be aware of one's feelings than not to be aware. But they are not always accurate guides to determining what is going on in the situation itself or what we should do about it. The issue is not to "get rid" of feelings. God created us to have feelings. But God also created us with a thinking brain and expects us to use it to understand what is going on and to determine how we will behave.

Groups of people, congregations, committees, and copastors get into greater emotional difficulty and confusion when they are not able to achieve a more thoughtful, objective stance within the emotional system, to see more clearly what is going on from the perspective of the bigger picture, and to think more rationally through the consequences of their possible actions. In other words, they behave foolishly.

DIFFERENTIATION AND WISDOM

The Old Testament emphasizes wisdom as a primary characteristic of a righteous person. This emphasis is especially clear in the early chapters of Proverbs, where wisdom is personified in feminine form and said to be desired above everything else. Jesus himself was held up as the embodiment and fulfillment of wisdom by many New Testament biblical authors.

Differentiation is equivalent to the biblical concept of wisdom, which is a quality independent of a person's intelligence quotient and educational degrees. Wisdom has to do with people's ability to effectively use what they know. Genuinely wise people tend to be better differentiated people; they have a more solid sense of self. Our image of the wise person as "calm, cool, and collected," even in the midst of a tumultuous situation, speaks to the fact that wisdom requires a lower level of chronic anxiety and a greater ability to think clearly in anxious situations.

Differentiation is the personal process that allows us to develop the kind of emotional skills we saw at work at Third Church. It is *the* basic requirement for good leadership in the church and the major marker that distinguishes better and poorer leaders.

Differentiation is not about knowing a lot of interpersonal skills, such as communication, problem solving, and how to be assertive. As a therapist, I "know" a great deal about these kinds of skills, but in the emotional heat of the moment, when I am acting out of fusion, I can easily lose what I know and react to the other person as if I had none of these skills. Differentiation is what it takes to consistently and effectively use these kinds of skills. Highly intelligent and well-educated people can still be highly fused. And relatively uneducated people can be better differentiated than people with a Ph.D.

A higher level of differentiation means a person has:

1. the ability to perceive more accurately the reality of situations, to not create threat that isn't really there, and to discern what is actually threatening and how;

2. the ability to identify his or her own opinions, beliefs, values, and commitments, and the principles of behavior that derive from these, as they are relevant to a particular situation;

3. the ability to think clearly and wisely about possible options for action and the likely consequences for each of these options;

4. and the ability to act flexibly within the situation on the basis of these perceptions, thoughts, and principles.

As differentiation increases within us, we are better able to define an emotionally separate self within the relationships we are a part of and to make choices about when, where, and how—and whether—to be emotionally close and connected to others. It gives us greater flexibility in how we will relate and respond to others and to the changing situations of life.

Differentiation brings with it a stronger sense of emotional well-being. There is less sense of others being a threat to us, even if they are angry with us. This greater comfort allows us to stay connected to the other because we do not need their acceptance, understanding, affirmation, praise, or agreement to feel okay. As a result, there is less sense that they are in charge of us, and less expectation that others will act, think, or feel in certain ways so that we will feel better.

At Third Church, each of the participants had feeling reactions to the upsetting situations of the morning, but they had enough ability to be in charge of these feelings so that their subjective responses did not run their behavior. Their thinking was less affected by their feelings. They knew what they were feeling but did not "feel compelled" to act on these feelings. The greater separateness between their thinking and feeling allowed them to make choices.

Differentiation is this ability to be in charge of self, even when others in the emotional field are actually trying to make us be different from how we are. We can keep our own direction and move at our own pace, according to our own assessment of the situation. Our compass is demagnetized and less affected by the emotional force field.

It was this kind of clarity that allowed people in the adult class at Third Church to discuss controversial issues without becoming highly argumentative or divisive. They were able to be open about their own beliefs, opinions, values, and commitments, without feeling done in or damaged by the significant ways others were different from them. They did not perceive differentness of others as a threat to their own emotional well-being or to their own choices about how to live their lives.

This stance allowed them to continue to learn from one another and to use the differentness of others to develop their own thinking and clarify their own views. They were even able to change their minds, at times, without this being seen as a good/bad thing where one "side" loses and the other wins.

DIFFERENTIATION AND THE CONGREGATION

Differentiation also allows people to be more comfortably connected and intimate with one another. Emotional movement either toward closeness or toward distance stirs up less of a sense of threat. Paradoxically, it seems, when there is less of a sense of desperate neediness for approval, love, and acceptance, people are able to be more themselves with one another and get closer. People hold more lightly the expectations of others and ideas about how they "should be" with us, and insist less on their expectations being fulfilled. There is, therefore, more likelihood of people arriving at a satisfactory solution to their relational difficulties.

As a more differentiated person, you may decide, for example, to cooperate with the group's wishes, even to make compromises of your beliefs, if that fits with a larger goal you have. But it is your decision, made on the basis of what makes sense to you, not on the basis of what others want; the wants of others are only one factor you take into consideration.

Greater differentiation in one or more individuals, above the average level in the group, is always a plus for any group. Not only is better thinking then available to the group, with less chance that the group will simply act out of the anxiety of the moment, but also better differentiated individuals are more emotionally available to groups. They are less emotionally distant from the group and stay in more responsible contact with the group. While the group may experience this more differentiated behavior as more challenging (as opposed to merely complying), the group will usually, after the anxiety of the situation is over, see the person as a resource to the group.

In the book *Family Evaluation* (New York, W. W. Norton & Co., 1988), Michael Kerr writes about the level of differentiation of a family. I have adapted his words here to show how they might apply to the church or other faith groups. With my changes, the quote would read this way:

> "The higher the level of differentiation of people in a church, synagogue, or faith group, the more they can cooperate, look out for one another's welfare, and stay in adequate emotional contact during stressful as well as calm periods. The lower the level of differentiation, the more likely the faith group, when stressed, will regress to selfish, aggressive, and avoidance behaviors; cohesiveness, altruism, and cooperativeness will break down." (adapted from p. 93)

The first sentence of the quote describes the way members at Third Church managed themselves on that difficult Sunday morning. The last sentence describes just exactly what we saw happen at Valley View church.

The higher the level of differentiation, on average, within a church (and among the leaders in particular):

1. the more that church will be able to maintain a sense of connection between members, regardless of the differences between them, and the more cohesive it will be;

2. the more the church will effectively work with a concern for one another's well-being, or the greater the love members will have for one another; and

3. the more the church will be able to work cooperatively to identify and accomplish common goals and objectives, and to pursue its mission.

A church board meeting composed of relatively well-differentiated board members like those at Third Church, for example, looks quite different from a board meeting of much less well-differentiated members. Whatever the topic before the board, even with a variety of beliefs and political positions among them, the discussion will be respectful, open, and constructive. Each board member will be able to articulate clearly his or her own position. Whatever passion is used when stating a position is not aimed at attacking the position of others, putting them down, or ridiculing them, but simply to indicate the depth of one's own beliefs.

The board members will also be able to listen well to one another, putting aside their own passion for the sake of being clear about what others are saying and what they believe. They will be curious about the different positions of others, ask questions that explore these differences, and use the thinking of others to stimulate and develop their own thinking and to learn. If they begin to be persuaded by the others and change their position, they do this comfortably and without a sense of humiliation at being wrong; it is just that their best thinking led them to a new position.

In the process of discussion, the various board members might discover common ground, a position they can all support. Or some members might be willing to compromise on their position for the sake of some larger principle that is important to them. Even if they are not able to arrive at some kind of agreement and end up with a split vote on an issue, they will be able to maintain a good emotional connection with one another.

Adaptability and flexibility are other ways to talk about the level of differentiation in a congregation. Due to the differences in their average level of differentiation, the leaders at Third Church were more adaptive than the leaders at Valley View to the challenge they faced on that Sunday morning and more flexible in how they managed their decision making.

Every church has a general or average level of flexibility, based primarily on the average level of differentiation of its members and particularly its leaders. The higher the average level of differentiation of the membership of a church, the more competently it will adapt to the needs of the present circumstances, and the greater flexibility it will show when accomplishing its goals and living out its Christian principles within the circumstances presented to it.

QUESTIONS

For Your Own Thinking

1. What is your personal definition of wisdom, and how does that compare with the ideas in this chapter?

2. How much do you find yourself blaming others, rather than taking responsibility for your own part in difficulties with others? Are you open with others about what you believe your part is?

3. To what extent are you able to take responsibility for your own feelings and behavior, rather than believing that others "make" you feel and behave the way you do?

4. To what extent do you blame God if circumstances in your life don't work out the way you would wish?

5. To what extent are you able to distinguish between opinions and facts?

6. When situations in your life become difficult, to what extent do you reactively focus on how others are or are not being, rather than proactively focusing on how you want to be in those situations?

7. How do you rate your ability to be flexible?

For Group Discussion

1. As you look at your congregation during times of higher anxiety, do you see it getting more caught up in the reactivity and foolishness of fusion, or being more reflective and able to operate out of the wisdom of differentiation? Give some examples.

2. What in particular seems to push your congregation toward fusion or differentiation?

3. From your perspective, how well is responsibility managed in your church?

4. From your perspective, what is the legitimate role of feelings in the life of faith and in the church, and how, if at all, do feelings become a problem?

5. Give some examples of times in the church of when people have been able to maintain a proactive, goal focus, rather than a reactive, "other" focus (when people have been able to operate at a higher level of differentiation).

6. How well are people in the church able to state their own position without attacking that of others, and how well are they able to listen to and understand the position of others?

7. On a scale of 1 to 10, how would you rate your church's adaptability and flexibility when resolving challenging situations (with 1 being extremely rigid and 10 being extremely flexible)? What specific incidents or behaviors led you to choose this score?

8. What other biblical stories or theological concepts seem to fit with and illustrate the idea of differentiation?

7

REACTIVITY IS MORE THAN REACTING

I entreat Euodia and I entreat Syntyche to agree in the Lord.
(Philipians 4:2)

Repay no one evil for evil, but take thought for what is noble in the sight of all. *(Romans 12:17)*

ANXIETY AND THE REACTIVE PROCESS IN THE CONGREGATION

When people begin to be anxious about the differences that exist in their community and their level of differentiation is relatively low, a certain predictable reactive process begins. Reactivity is the emotional expression of people's sense of threat. After you have been in a congregation long enough, you can begin to predict which people will get upset about which issues and in what way they will be upset. These predictions, or understandings of others' sensitivities, then become part of the decision-making process of the leadership ("We won't do this/that because he/she/they will get upset").

While generally speaking making a point of not upsetting others for no good reason might be a good policy to follow, making all decisions on the basis of this principle is not good policy. A lot of the biblical story would not have happened if not upsetting others had been the principle that guided leadership.

When we begin to feel anxious, one of the first questions we usually ask is whose fault it is. If the answer turns out to be "It's me" or "I'm wrong," then we may try to shape up or change in order to fit in better with the others. Many preachers and teachers hope for this response every Sunday morning.

This response of, "It's me," can work fine. Focusing on trying to shape oneself up in some important way can lead to growth or increased competency or to a more mature Christian life. But to achieve this outcome, it has to happen as a result of a more or less autonomous decision to pursue this change. Others may want to see this change take place, but we must want the change, too.

But if the response is "It's me," and the change that is being asked for is not something we want, we may make the changes reluctantly out of fear of abandonment ("If I am not the way he wants, he will leave me," or not care for me, not accept me, and so forth). In this case, the changes can lead to a loss of self and to depression. (Depression usually involves a loss of self to someone or something else.)

However, most people decide that the fault lies with the other person when significant, anxiety-stirring difference is discovered. Take, for an example, any issue in your church that people are divided about right now. People on either side of the question may tend to see people on the other side as "the problem." They will do and say whatever they can to focus on the wrongness of the other's position and to develop the best arguments for their own position. They get reactively focused on the other as the source of their own anxious discomfort.

This automatic reactivity develops out of a belief that "closeness is sameness." It leads to increased efforts to change the other from their "different" stance to our own ("If the other will only think, feel, be like me, then I can feel okay"). If left unchecked, the reactivity will lead to nasty and mean-spirited church fights and ultimately to splits in the congregation or denomination as the one experiencing the pressure to change begins to distance.

At Valley View, the apparently trivial feud between Marie Fontana and Harry Harding over the placement of flowers in the sanctuary on Sunday mornings is the kind of issue that can lead to people leaving a committee or the church. Most church leaders have seen a conflict of this sort in which something that seems inconsequential becomes a big deal to the participants.

The issue, of course, is not really over the placement of the flowers. The issue is that both Marie and Harry have their sense of self invested in their official positions and the authority to decide about the placement of the flowers. Maintaining our sense of self is a major priority for all of us, and we can become anxious when it is threatened. The differences between the parties become important because they have invested themselves in the issue.

The need to have one's sense of self bolstered by a position of authority, or to get respect from others because of one's authority, represents unfinished business from the person's past. Being seen as "right," "good," "correct," "the best," or whatever is about propping ourselves up with recognition from others. These unresolved issues from the past lead us to look for respect (or praise or recognition or whatever) from others so we can feel okay; then we get angry or depressed if we don't get what we expect.

A similar kind of "petty issue" at Third Church might have developed into a problem had the people been reactive during the discussions about using live sheep and goats in the Christmas pageant. Some thought "it was a really nice touch," and others could only see the problems involved in doing it. But since people did not have their selves invested in one position or the other or in whose "right" it was to make the decision, they were able to discuss the issue in much more practical terms. Who would get the animals and return them? Who would look after them at the church and clean up after them? Would the animals scare the children? Was it worth all the energy? The committee discussion turned out to be mostly about who was willing to be responsible for what if they did get live animals and about getting firm commitments.

PATTERNS OF REACTIVITY

People respond to the pressure for sameness with one of four common patterns of reactivity. The one thing the four patterns have in common is that they are all strategies for distancing and not dealing directly with the experience of threat. They are just ways of trying to deal with the anxiety.

Compliance

One kind of reactivity is *compliance*. This compliance is an outward and perfunctory appearance of going along with the wishes of the other, while inwardly (maybe unconsciously) resenting being "forced" into this behavior.

Reactive compliance often leaves the one requesting the changes confused or frustrated. This is because the compliant one agrees to make a change, but the change never actually happens, or it is done incorrectly or poorly. The compliant one seems so nice that it is difficult to confront him or her with the actual lack of change.

Compliance was not the most common response that Sunday morning at Valley View. A small example is Roy's agreement with Marie to take up the flower placement issue with Harry and the worship committee. Roy had no intent of doing this because he didn't care one way or the other, but he didn't really want to deal with Marie about it. This is how the appearance of compliance can be a form of distancing.

Later on, Marie might ask Roy what was decided about the flowers at the worship committee meeting, and he might make all kinds of excuses without ever saying directly to Marie that he really wasn't willing to make this his issue with the committee. He wouldn't state his position on the issue, but would appear to go along with Marie, which he would probably also do with Harry if Harry asked him to talk to Marie. Both Marie and Harry would end up feeling confused about what was going on.

Rebellion

A second pattern of reactivity is open *rebellion,* as opposed to the hidden rebellion of compliance. The rebellious person makes a point of doing or saying exactly the opposite of whatever is requested. The rebel has a strong sense of his or her own freedom and "rights," and is sensitive to any demands or requests that seem unfair.

The problem for rebels is not being able to get on with life and their own direction and goals. Thus they paradoxically also lose self. Hard-core, committed rebels are so busy making sure that no one can make any claims on them or tell them what to do or how to live that they spend all their time reacting to others, rather than acting for themselves. Their goals end up being to do the opposite of what they are told or expected to do. They have no goals of their own.

This way of trying to create some emotional distance and to get a sense of emotional separateness and autonomy keeps rebels pretty dependent on others. Rebels need others who will be authorities; without authorities, rebels lack direction.

At Valley View, one of the best examples of the rebel is Larry Lambert, the custodian, and Stu is his authority. Larry's statements are almost a direct invitation to Stu to be authoritarian with him, which Stu is; both of them only end up getting more frustrated.

Power Struggle

The third pattern is the *power struggle.* This strategy certainly has some of the rebel in it, but rather than doing just the negative side

("I'm not going to do that!"), it includes another side: "but you better do this!" In the power struggle, each side evaluates the other as wrong and tells the other what to do. In a sense, both parties become pursuers (as well emotional distancers with regard to openness about self).

Frustration and anger are the major subjective experience for people engaged in a power struggle. They are so focused on changing the other that, like the rebel, they don't get on with their own life. They tend to think that life with the other person would be just great if only the other would shape up and do what he or she is "supposed to do." Power struggle talk is full of accusations, blaming, and fault finding, and every little slight, hurt, and inadequacy that ever happened—or was imagined to happen—in the relationship can get brought into every argument.

This ongoing dynamic keeps the antagonists involved with each other over time. The power struggle has the dual advantage of allowing the two to keep some distance in the relationship but also to stay connected. The relationship may well have interludes of peace, but this happens only when people find some sameness that they both enjoy.

There were many power struggles at Valley View. Roy certainly has this kind of relationship with both Stu McGuire and Harry Harding in the church, and with Janet Whalley in the day-care program. In each relationship, both parties focus on how the other should be different and how they are perfectly justified taking their own position.

Both Stu and Harry had once been big supporters of calling Roy as the pastor of the church. They wanted a "take-charge kind of guy" as their pastor. The previous pastor had been a very "weak" administrator from their point of view. But Stu and Harry thought that Roy would exercise his authority in the same way and for the same purposes as they would. This was their fantasy of sameness. And Roy liked the fact that they wanted someone who would come in and exercise "leadership" (which is how he would have described his behavior). Roy certainly had the same fantasy of sameness, but the question for those involved in power struggles always is, Whose sameness will it be?

Emotional Distancing

The fourth reactive strategy for dealing with the pressure for sameness is overt physical or *emotional distancing*, as opposed to the more covert distancing that is used in the other three strategies. In this case, people just refuse to engage with the other; they make themselves unavailable. People using this strategy may stop attending either the worship service or a group they were once active in, or they may show up but not be as active a participant as they once were, or they may stop talking to the person with whom they were once more involved.

People take this kind of distancing stance when they don't know what else to do. They may have tried everything they know how to do to relate to the other and maintain a sense of self, but once they get the idea that there is no way to be an acceptable self with the other and that a relationship with the other would only be on the other's terms, then distancing overtly is the only way they know to maintain a sense of self.

This is when people begin to say things, if they say anything, like, "I need some time away from the church; I am just too involved" or "I need some space, some breathing room" or "There are just so many other things going on in my life right now that I have to deal with." Most often in the church people will just disappear and give up on the relationship.

Janet Whalley was threatening to use overt distancing as a way to fight with Roy by saying she would move her day-care program to another church. In this case, distancing can still be a part of the power struggle strategy. But this withdrawal is often the ultimate trump card in the power struggle relationship: "If I can't have it my way with you, then I will leave." The threat of abandonment is especially powerful in mutually dependent relationships. But once the other person sees the threat as just another way to fight, he or she tends not to take it seriously and might come back, as Roy did, with some version of "Go ahead! Who needs you? I don't care!"

The threat of leaving, however, is a different ploy from actually leaving. This is the strategy that Maureen Niven decided to use with Roy and the church. With her resignation, she moved from somewhat compliant, covert distancing to overt distancing. Throughout her life, she had experienced people leaning on her and demanding that she be a particular way for them. She'd had lots of struggles with depression in her life, and finally she was deciding to give up on ever expecting any recognition or support from others. She was going to resign from all of these involvements. Then, she thought, she would be free.

The problem for Maureen, and for anyone who relates the way she does, is that the same dynamic is going to follow her wherever she goes. She tends to see it as being about how other people are with her, rather than how she is with them. Her unchanging perception, and the resulting strategy, will leave her as unhappy as always, whoever she's with, and ultimately she will end up lonely. Her life will become one resignation after another.

When we can hang in and work on being a self with emotionally powerful others, then our "resignations," whenever they happen, will be about getting on to new things in life or tackling new challenges, not about getting away from people and places where we feel defeated and done in and unable to be a self.

If you, as a church leader, find people using one or more of these four patterns with you, rather than focusing on "their problem," look at how you are a part of the problem, how you are pursuing people with a "sameness" mentality, or how you might be perceived to be doing this.

You won't be able to change others or keep them from using these patterns with you, but if you focus on and can change your part in the reactive process, they may need to use these patterns less often and may find ways to be more direct and open with you. However, and here is the catch, you have to be willing to let go of the idea that they should be different from how they are, more like you.

The following pastoral counseling story illustrates how these patterns of reactivity look in a close relationship dealing with issues of faith. A young man in his late twenties came to me in my pastoral counseling practice complaining that his mother was putting a lot of pressure on him to attend what she called "a more gospel-centered church." He had moved from home about a year before, and now mom, who lived two hundred miles away, called two or three times a week, saying she was praying for him to see the error of his ways. She wanted him to go back to the "true" church and leave the "liberal" one he was now attending. It was clear that he was not going to attend the church his mother wanted him to. He was full of a mixture of guilt and anger at his mother and wanted her "to get off my back and leave me alone."

His mom seemed to be pushing a "closeness as sameness" agenda, and he was saying, in effect, "We are just too different to be close." His sense of self was significantly threatened in her presence. He had used all four of the reactive processes to attempt to deal with her. The family looked like this.

Family diagram

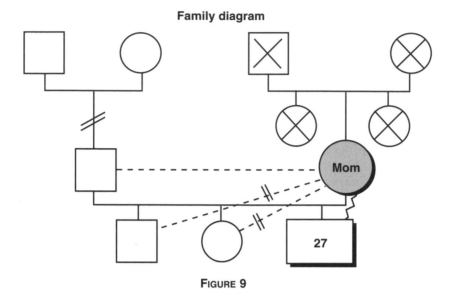

FIGURE 9

I asked a number of questions about the family. Dad was heavily involved with work and was rarely home. My client's two older siblings had moved away from home with lots of anger at mom over the same kind of issues and had vowed—after giving up on trying to make her change—never to have anything to do with her again. My client, the youngest child, had been a kind of companion and confidant for mom up to the time he moved away. He had been compliant and gone to her church. He thought when he moved that he could "become my own person." However, his mother's calls and letters haunted him.

Contrary to his expectations and what his current pastor had suggested, I did not encourage him to cut off (like his siblings) and completely distance from mother or to angrily confront her. I asked him to make several visits back home and to spend time getting to know mom, rather than arguing with her about the right church to attend.

For example, I said that whenever mom expressed concern about his faith, that he should take this as an opportunity to get to know her and to ask her about how she came to be so devout and committed in her faith. I suggested that he tell her about his doubts and struggles with issues of faith, and ask her how she became so certain in her faith. I suggested that he should praise her for her faith (something that he did, in fact, genuinely appreciate about her) and say that he wished he could get to this kind of certainty (which he did wish for himself).

He thought my suggestions were crazy and that they would just entangle him in mom's clutches all the more, but since he felt so desperate and could see no other options, he decided to give them a try.

He came back from each visit feeling much better about himself and his relationship with his mother. As he asked her about the certainty of her faith, she gradually began to be open about her doubts and her own struggles with faith. He showed interest in her own growing-up years in her family of origin and how she had experienced her life. He learned things about her he had never known before.

She stopped calling and writing so much and stopped talking about what church her son was attending. He felt that he had begun to get himself emotionally separate from his mother and was more able to be himself with her. This helped him to feel closer to her than he could ever remember in his life, while at the same time he felt freer to live life as it made sense to him. It was a kind of liberation for him.

What happened? My theory was that mom had panicked about being alone and thought she could hang on to some semblance of her son through the faith/church issue. She was experiencing abandonment (death of members of her own family, distant husband, cutoff children) and began to pursue her son intensely, using church as the focus issue. The more son distanced and cut off from her, the more anxious she became. She used the same approach she did with each of the other family members, inducing guilt in order to try to keep some kind of connection. She didn't understand that this tactic only fed her family's emotional distance from her.

My theory was that if the son could stop getting caught up in these defensive knots with his mother and start to pursue her, rather than distance from her (the distancing only bringing about more pursuit from her), and if he could reach out to her with some interest in her as a person, rather than defending himself, then mom's level of anxiety would go down and she would stop her pursuit and pushing for "sameness in faith" with him. And that is exactly what happened.

Not all faith issues are really just about closeness and distance. Issues of faith and belief have a substance of their own, which we must take seriously as Christians. But in this case, the faith issues were a foil for both mother's and son's efforts to deal with their anxiety. The strong emotional system issues were getting in the way of their being able to talk about anything of any consequence, including issues of faith and belief. By taking this new direction, the son felt like he was more consistently living out his own professed faith.

QUESTIONS

For Your Own Thinking

1. How predictable do you think you are to those who know you? Do they know when and how you will become reactive?

2. When things start going wrong in the church, to what extent do you find yourself moving into a blaming stance? Do you have any particular people you tend to focus on?

3. In what ways do you reactively comply with the wishes of others in the church? In what ways do you rebel? In what ways do you become involved in a power struggle? When, and from whom do you distance, and how?

4. What are some of your best methods for stimulating reactivity in others?

For Group Discussion

1. If your church had a favorite reactive style as a congregation, what might it be?

2. In what ways might you, as a group of leaders, be inadvertently arousing reactivity within members of the congregation at the present time? What are some alternative ways of being that might avoid stimulating reactivity in the members?

3. What principled positions do you believe it is important to take in the church in your current circumstances, even though others in the congregation or in the community may be upset and become reactive? Can you see better or worse ways of doing this? What are they?

4. Which biblical stories demonstrate emotional reactivity?

8

THE FOUR FUNCTIONAL STYLES
OF CONGREGATIONAL LIFE

Welcome one another, therefore, as Christ has welcomed you.
(Romans 15:7)

. . . holding the form of religion but denying the power of it.
(2 Timothy 3:5)

BRINGING IT ALL TOGETHER

This chapter provides a graphic key showing how the elements discussed so far fit together. Relationships, of course, are much more multifaceted than any graph can show, but the graph provides a theoretical perspective for thinking about the nature of emotional relationships in your church.

When the two primary life forces of togetherness and individuality, and the two relational needs for closeness to and distance from others are looked at along with the two primary processes for dealing with them—fusion and differentiation, the result can be graphed in the following way:

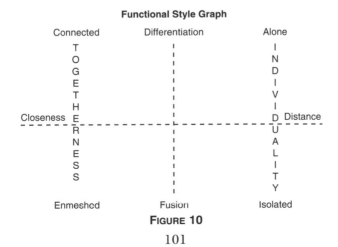

Functional Style Graph

	Connected	Differentiation	Alone
	T		I
	O		N
	G		D
	E		I
	T		V
	H		I
Closeness	E		D	Distance
	R		U
	N		A
	E		L
	S		I
	S		T
			Y
	Enmeshed	Fusion	Isolated

FIGURE 10

There are two primary axes on the functional style graph, expressed as broken lines: the vertical axis of differentiation/fusion; and the horizontal axis of emotional closeness and distance. Both dimensions are bounded by and heavily influenced by the basic life forces of togetherness and individuality.

If you think of the two primary axis as moveable crosshairs, then the point where they intersect for each person, and for groups of people generally, at any given moment, will be within one of the four quadrants of the graph, which I have named enmeshed, isolated, connected, and alone.

The graph shows that there are two significantly different ways to be with or close to others, and two significantly different ways to be distant or apart from others, depending on whether one is moving in a more differentiated or a more fused direction. I will briefly describe the resulting four quadrants, what they look like behaviorally, how they are experienced by people in an emotional system, and some of the implications of each quadrant for faith and church congregational life.

ENMESHED

The functional style of the lower left quadrant is *enmeshed fusion*.

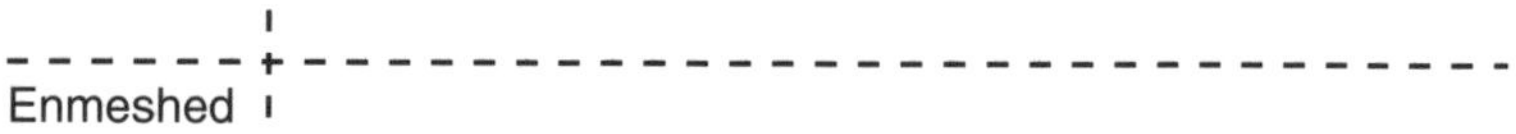

FIGURE 11

In the extreme, when individuals, families, and congregations are operating within this area, they have trouble knowing where one person's boundaries stop and those of others start. The self of each is so fused with the other that when one itches, the other scratches. People think, feel, and speak for each other. Ask one a question and the other answers. They read one another's mind. Emotionally they seem like a stuck together blob with little sense that any of them have a life of their own, apart from the other. Murray Bowen's original term for this phenomenon was quite descriptive, despite its clinical sound: "undifferentiated family ego mass."

The fear of abandonment, of being left alone in the world, would be the most powerful motivating force for people when operating in this quadrant, and they would do everything they could, including giving up major parts of self, to avoid this outcome. They have a deep-seated need to be loved, accepted, approved of, and guided by others; or, conversely, to provide this for others. Their emotional life soars when they are praised, and crashes when they are criticized.

In the lowest levels of this quadrant, there is practically no capacity for autonomous functioning. Indeed, such independent functioning gets defined by people in this quadrant as "selfish" and "uncaring," and they have very little sense of how the invasion of other people's boundaries and the subversion of their own functioning is actually an unloving and uncaring act.

Here are some of the characteristics we might display when our functional style is in this quadrant.

- We are on guard for any sign of interpersonal threat, always watching for any minor slight as well as overt attacks.
- We tend to think others are responsible for our experience, and/or we are responsible for theirs.
- We have a sensitivity to criticism, which creates a sense of feeling damaged or harmed by it, so we tailor our lives to avoid criticism, and we resent or fear those who give it.
- We seek approval and praise, perhaps believing we need this to be happy, and like an addict feel miserable if we don't get it.
- We may work hard to please others, getting our feelings of okayness from pleasing them.
- We become overly concerned about our position in the hierarchy and whether we are receiving our due recognition or about whether our authority is being respected.
- We may have a reaction to the difficult circumstances of others that leads us to be overly sympathetic by trying to make things better for them, rescuing them, when they actually have to do the job for themselves.
- Conversely, we may think that others should be doing more for us, even when we are actually capable of doing for ourselves. (We see others as responsible for our happiness).

Church groups that regularly operate within this quadrant can be of any ideological persuasion; they can be radical right and fundamentalist, or radical left and revolutionary, or anywhere in between.

The style of functioning for any of the quadrants is not related to specific content of faith or of political belief.

The development of our own personal faith is difficult when we are in this quadrant. The reaction of others to our beliefs will have a powerful modifying impact, so we play down or do not voice all our beliefs. We might even change our beliefs in order to fit in with the prevailing beliefs of the emotional system, or of some subsystem within the larger system, or with the beliefs of the leadership of the system whose approval we want.

One woman in counseling spoke of the difficulty she was having in her church. She thought of herself as a strong and committed Christian, but she knew that she did not actually believe what others in her church said they believed, and she knew that if she said so, they would reject her. She felt deeply needy of their friendship and fellowship, so she verbally professed the same beliefs and was seen as being "like them." But she decided that she wasn't known by these people, and they could not truly be her friends if they didn't actually know her.

As it turned out, in this case, she was right. As she took the risk to say what she believed (hoping both to stay connected to them and to be true to herself), others did become cool and distance from her, and they would not talk with her about this distancing. She saw that the friendship was a sham, and that people were more invested in an anxious "togetherness as sameness." She moved her membership to a church where she felt better connected with others and there was a greater comfort with a difference in beliefs.

Another example of enmeshed fusion would be a church community that incorporates into its own Christian faith some beliefs that are popular in the culture it is a part of, and fuses these together in order to meet some larger emotional goals, like nationalism. In some Christian circles, there is a sense that God and the state are at an equal level, and devotion to one must be balanced with an equal devotion to the other.

Another emotional goal could be "the family." Family togetherness was not an important theme in the life and teaching of Jesus. If all of his sayings about family relationships in the gospels were put together, the vast majority present a fairly negative view of family. Certainly he was not against the family, per se, but he was aware that in his culture it had become an idol, and he believed no worldly human structure could have the same claim on humanity as did the relationship with God.

The language of faith is sometimes used to rationalize and support our fused enmeshment impulses in inappropriate ways. Many people would swear that the well-known aphorism, "The family that prays together stays together," is a biblical verse. (And when they discover it is not, they say, "Well, it should be"). The phrase celebrates family togetherness as a top Christian priority, as if the point of prayer is family togetherness, and ignores the teachings of Jesus, which say just the opposite.

Walter Lippmann once said, "When all think alike, no one thinks very much." That is a good description of some enmeshed church systems. There will be a low level of tolerance for differences in thinking, feeling, and doing. The leadership will tend toward authoritarian, autocratic, rigid, legalistic, and dogmatic stances. They will not allow any questioning of the principles of faith or of the authority of the leadership.

Faith groups in this quadrant have an entangled and intense emotional atmosphere about them. Even in spite of the appearance that they are "gifted" in many ways and appear to be "successful" by many standards, the emotional morass of their communal life will ultimately defeat their ability to maintain a unified and effective way of working together. So much energy will go into the internal life of the group (for example, spending time "processing" their relationships, or engaging in regular quarrels and fights) and the turmoil centered on this, that the group will ultimately be unable to accomplish its goals.

This kind of church eventually develops a major symptom of some sort—a "church split" is one of the most common. Another difficulty could be some dramatic form of acting out by an otherwise well-liked and usually charismatic church leader (who, for example, sexually abuses a parishioner), which will then lead to divisions within the group.

ISOLATED

The functional style of the lower right quadrant is that of *isolated fusion*.

- + - - - - -
                                                             ¦ Isolated

FIGURE 12

To be both fused and isolated sounds wrong according to our usual understanding of these words. When we are functioning in this quadrant, we are so allergic or reactive to closeness that we attempt to maintain a sense of self by staying distant. The immature management of the life forces leads to a sense of individuality that excludes others or that sees others as the enemy of self.

Distance from any sort of "too close" emotional involvement is seen as the solution. Most young adults, male and female, have had this kind of reaction to one or both of their parents at some point. In this quadrant, we think the only way we can be ourselves is to be away from the one(s) we think of as emotionally powerful for us. The same reaction happens frequently in marriage, in some very intense friendships, and sometimes in relation to our church community.

Some people go from relationship to relationship, leaving each one at the point that it begins to be "too intense" according to their level of sensitivity. Bowen called these people "relationship nomads." They can stay in a relationship only as long as it does not become too emotionally intense. When it reaches that point, they have to leave as a way to try to hang on to self. The magnetic force of fusion is still there, but the poles have switched to repulsion rather than the attraction of enmeshment.

Church members operating out of a more isolated style will have tenuous connections with one another, and a church in this quadrant will be weakly connected to other churches. Or such a church could be strongly isolated from the world around it and perhaps deeply enmeshed within its boundaries. Cults often function in this way.

These ways of being vary over time and from relationship to relationship. A very dependent, shy, and even clinging younger boy could grow into a highly rebellious, defiant, and distancing adolescent. Whereas formerly he sought to please his parents and conform to their wishes (thus maintaining a fused closeness with them), later he seeks to upset them and flaunts his refusal to obey them (maintaining an equally fused distance from them).

Nothing has really changed in terms of the power of fusion for him or the parents; it is just acted out differently. He will probably become just as emotionally dependent and conforming with his peers as he used to be with his parents. Now he wants to get the friends' approval and is fearful of their rejection.

Another form of emotional distancing and isolation is to stay in the relationship but to work hard at not allowing any differences to emerge into the open and keeping everything nonconflictual and calm. Attempting to keep the level of disruption low can sap the vitality of a relationship. Boredom then becomes an important factor in the relationship. There is a sterile quality that keeps life uneventful and unexciting. Some people in churches, and sometimes whole churches, run their life this way.

It is not unusual for some people to try to deal with the power of their family of origin by moving thousands of miles away and having as little as possible to do with them for as long as possible. These people might also move from one church to another. While this certainly gives us some immediate sense of relief, it does not get us out of the fused place. And we carry our own magnetized force field around with us wherever we go, so we can be just as reactive in other contemporary emotional relationships. As Bowen once said, "Time and distance do not fool an emotional system."

Some people in this quadrant refuse to have anything to do with church or any religion or with group life of any sort. Some of these people even become "religiously" antireligious. They may simply have a Scrooge-like, "Bah, Humbug" stance, or they may more actively fight against and attack anyone who approaches them or impinges upon them with a significant faith perspective.

The famous reclusive Howard Hughes is one extreme example of the "rugged individualist" who could typify this style of functioning, cut off from all family members. He was a man who gradually grew more isolated from even friends over the years, having no meaningful personal relationships by the end of his life, becoming increasingly suspicious of others, and fearing "infection" by germs from others.

More differentiated church leaders can understand that the distancing is the other person's way of trying to gain emotional comfort and safety, to lower his/her level of anxiety, and to regain a sense of being in charge of self. In any contact they have with this distancing person, they will be sensitive to that issue, and have that person's sense of safety as a priority. Good leaders are people who know how to create a safe enough atmosphere in which people feel safe emotionally.

CONNECTED

The *differentiated connected* corner of the graph, however, is significantly different from the first two quadrants.

```
Connected  ¦
- - - - - ┼ - - - - - - - - - - - - - - - - - - - - - - - - - - - - - - - -
          ¦
```

FIGURE 13

More differentiated closeness allows people to develop a sense of connection, unity, intimacy, and mutual understanding without loss of self for either party. Connected people can be attentive to and care for one another. Differentiated closeness allowed the Good Samaritan (considered a foreigner in Israel, and therefore considered unclean by some Jewish standards) to take pity on the Israelite man who had been attacked by robbers, while the man's own country-men (who should have been "close") passed him by (distantly, "on the other side of the road").

In better differentiated people, the togetherness force is experi-enced as an attraction to and interest in others, rather than a deep yearning neediness for others, or for their love, acceptance, and sup-port (as in the enmeshed quadrant). This kind of connection allows us to enjoy each other, to celebrate the good things we experience in life, none of which are solely of our own doing but all of which come to us from beyond ourselves.

However, the critical issue in this kind of closeness is the ability to maintain a sense of self, of being in charge of self, while in close emo-tional contact with others. When there is a higher level of differen-tiation, we are less governed by the sensitivities listed in the enmeshed quadrant above. There is a greater sense of thinking through and deciding how self wants to be, and then, nonreactively, being able to follow through with that, even if others disapprove or do not coop-erate with us.

When people can be connected with one another and maintain a sense of self, there will be a higher level of ability to think through challenges and difficulties facing the group; they will be able to be open and clear with one another and attentive to one another; there will be a higher level of cooperation; and each will be responsible for self's own part in the process.

These sorts of connections can happen across hierarchical lines, as well, but people's level in the hierarchy will be deemphasized. And leadership will not so much reside in one person, according to his or her official position, as much as shift around to various people depending on the topic, area of expertise, and so forth. In a well-differentiated system, there would be a lower level of threat in people higher in the hierarchy and those who are lower around their particular place in the hierarchy, and there would be a lower level of competitiveness between members of the group as well.

People in this quadrant are free to allow themselves to get caught up in group worship or rituals and enjoy the togetherness of these activities, but they have no sense that these subjective spiritual experiences inhibit the need for objectivity if the occasion should call for it. In other words, better differentiated people are free to operate from either a thinking or a feeling position.

A better differentiated faith group will have, for the most part, well-defined, consistent beliefs. The majority of the members in the church will behave in a way that fits with these expressed beliefs. Since the group will not be ashamed of its beliefs, it will neither respond to pressure from public groups to change these beliefs nor shape its beliefs in order to win public support.

At the same time, the church group will always be open to dialogue, to new information or evidence, and will not use reason simply to defend a dogmatic position. There will be a firmness of belief without being rigid. And there will be a willingness to be in contact with critics of the group's beliefs, listen to their positions, and carefully take their comments into account.

These people will relate comfortably to authorities and are respectful of the hierarchies of the faith group. Power, authority, and hierarchy are recognized as simple organizational and political realities, not evils that have to be fought. These realities are known to have their limitations. And, while one never places too much expectation in appointed leaders' ability to deliver because of the diffuseness of responsibility in such structures, group members will respect the chain of command, and members and leaders will do their part to keep open communication up and down the chain.

ALONE

The skills that are drawn upon to achieve a more connected and differentiated quality, a sense of closeness with others, include those of the upper right hand quadrant, the *differentiated alone* functional style.

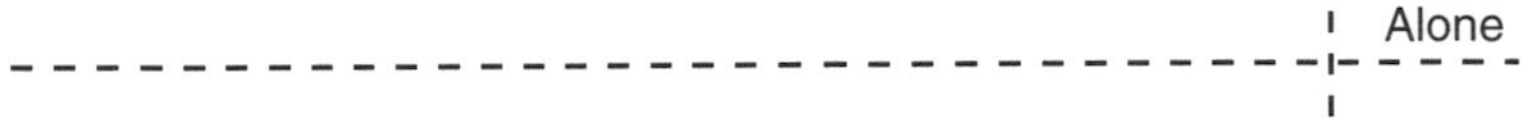

Alone

FIGURE 14

When the situation calls for it, people with a well-differentiated sense of their own individuality have the ability and, especially, the courage to stand alone, without any emotional support from others and without needing praise or recognition for what they do. They do not fear criticism, seek to avoid it, or look for approval and support for the positions they take. They do not need the cooperation of others in order to be a solid self.

This does not mean they will never feel the "loneliness" of abandonment; it simply means they will not be governed by it. At least three times, we see these feelings in Jesus: (1) in the Garden of Gethsemane, before he is arrested, where he scolds the disciples for their inability to "watch" with him in the aloneness of what he must do; (2) as the disciples abandon and deny him in the whirlwind of confusion surrounding his arrest; (3) on the cross when he cries out, asking why God has abandoned him. The hours on the cross were a time of utter aloneness for Jesus, who had experienced so profoundly the presence of God.

Generally, unlike the isolated person who operates out of fusion and reactivity and needs distance from others, we do not set out to be alone. Aloneness is not a goal for the better differentiated person. But we recognize that this could be the possible outcome of our actions and are not surprised by it. When acting on our principles and beliefs, and being true to our own understanding of what God asks of us, we may feel very alone; no one may support us; they may even mock us for our beliefs.

There is a kind of aloneness we may seek. That is solitude. We do not seek this sort of time apart from others reactively, against others, but proactively, as a way to clarify our own thinking, beliefs, goals, values, and so forth, in order that we can better connect with people. Solitude is about getting to know ourselves better, so we are clearer about what we have to bring to others. Solitude is a way to cultivate perspective and objectivity.

Taking time to be alone in solitude, or in prayer, may help us to nurture an attitude of gratitude, to become more tender, affectionate, loving, and to develop a gracious stance toward those we are close to. It may help us more honestly face our own foibles and shortcomings, and to face the painful failures of our lives. And it is a way to begin to make solid plans for our lives and to focus more on how we want to be.

Spiritually, the individual believer in the upper right hand quadrant will be capable of defining self's own beliefs and values, thinking these through over time. The individual is comfortable saying, "I believe . . . I think . . . I feel . . . I will, or will not, do . . ." without checking to see if these beliefs are acceptable to some other authority.

They may certainly be people of feeling and passion, but these subjective emotional experiences do not run their lives. When necessary they are able to step back and regain the more objective view and think situations through.

They will be people of action. With a better developed and stronger sense of self, people can act in ways that enhance their own welfare, without impinging or encroaching on the welfare of others or functioning at the expense of others. They will be with others on the basis of their own beliefs, principles, goals, and values, rather than simply on the basis of what others want. They will be fully responsible for self and will not engage in behaviors that foster or participate in the irresponsibility of others.

There will be greater consistency between professed beliefs and actual behavior. Words and action will match one another. Biblically, this is a characteristic of God. In both the first chapters of Genesis and the first verses of the Gospel of John, we see that God's words and actions are one and the same.

We see this ability to stand alone time and time again in the life of Jesus, of Paul, and of many other biblical personalities in both the Old and the New Testaments. It was this ability that allowed Martin Luther to say to his church superiors, "Here I stand, I can do no other," when they asked him to recant what they thought were his radical and heretical positions.

It was not Luther's intent to separate himself from the church. It was his intent to define what for him was correct belief. Coming from a more fused, togetherness-as-sameness, or enmeshed, orientation, the church fathers threatened him with separation and excommunication for holding to these beliefs. He had to have the emotional courage and ability to stand alone as they followed through on their threats and excommunicated him from the church as a heretic.

A THIRD DIMENSION

All two-dimensional graphs, like the one with the four quadrants, vastly oversimplify things. Books limit us to the two dimensions. We need our imagination to understand the third dimension, the element of time. If we could see individuals or a church as they move through time, we would see them taking different positions on the graph—at different points in their lives, in different relationships, around different circumstances or situations, and with various levels of emotional intensity and anxiety.

The fluctuations and movements from one quadrant to another, from better differentiated to more fused functioning, will depend primarily on the level of anxiety within the individuals and in the church group generally. As anxiety goes up, the functioning of people will move further into the lower, fused portion of the graph. And if they have high levels of chronic anxiety, they will tend to stay there for longer periods of time, perhaps for all of their life.

Given enough stress, even well differentiated people can begin to function in more fused ways. Given enough calmness and lack of upsetting situations, more fused and chronically anxious people can look pretty well differentiated.

QUESTIONS

For Your Own Thinking

1. In what quadrant of the graph do you think you personally spend most of your time?

2. Under what circumstances and with what people do you tend to vary from this typical quadrant?

3. If you typically are in the lower half of the graph (either enmeshed or isolated) can you identify what aspects of fusion help to keep you there?

4. Nearly all of us have a certain amount of fear of either abandonment or engulfment; what circumstances or people tend to get these feelings stimulated in you?

5. Can you think of relationships where there has been significant differences between you and the other person and yet you have been able to remain comfortably connected with and interested in the other person? What in you helped you to do this?

6. Can you think of a time when you have had to stand alone because of your beliefs? How comfortable were you with this position and what in you helped you to do this?

7. Assuming that stronger faith and a higher level of differentia-

tion go hand in hand, what qualities of differentiation within you have helped you to become a person of greater faith?

For Group Discussion

1. In what specific ways might you see your own church as either enmeshed or isolated?

2. Can you think of any ways in your church in which faith and culture have been enmeshed, or some aspect of culture has been made into an idolatry?

3. To what extent, if at all, has nationalism or family togetherness been made an idol in your church?

4. Are there any ways in which your church has distanced from the culture around it, and has isolated itself from the realities of people's lives in that culture?

5. In terms of the graph where would you put your church in relation to your denomination, and in relation to the authority it seeks to exercise? What factors enter into your thinking about this?

6. To what extent have members of the group found solitude helpful in getting clearer about one's own beliefs, goals, commitments, values, and sense of self?

7. Looking at the lives of various apostles as they are described in the New Testament, what stories reflect them functioning in different quadrants of the graph?

9

TRIANGLES IN THE CONGREGATION

"Let him who is without sin among you be the first to throw a stone at her."　　　　　　　　　　　　　　*(John 8:7)*

Rather, speaking the truth in love.　　　　　　　　*(Ephesians 4:15)*

WHAT IS A TRIANGLE?

When Marie at Valley View was upset that Harry had moved the flowers in the sanctuary, she went to Roy to complain. She believed she would be unable to influence Harry herself, so she went to Roy, a "higher" authority, for help, support, and backup in her fight with Harry. She created an instant triangle between herself, Harry, and Roy. She and Roy were in the close corners, and Harry was in the outside, more distant position.

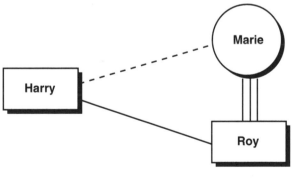

FIGURE 15

Marie asked Roy to take responsibility for her conflict with Harry instead of dealing with it herself. She felt more comfortable talking to Roy, whom she believed felt the same about Harry.

114

By agreeing with Marie (to her face) instead of saying "I won't get into this, this is between you and Harry," Roy becomes part of the triangle. In this case, Roy does not actually agree with her but wants to maintain the closer connection with her, so he does not say that he disagrees. The next time he is with Harry, Roy might say something like, "You know Marie has this bee in her bonnet about the flowers thing, but I wouldn't take it too seriously, Harry, she just doesn't like anyone infringing on her territory. She'll get over it; I'll talk to her." By doing this, Roy moves the points of the triangle so that he and Harry have the closer connection and Marie is on the outside point.

Because Roy wants to maintain a kind of closeness with Marie, he never says anything to her directly about what he really thinks. In the end, everyone is confused and cannot trust who is saying what to whom and for what purpose.

It Takes More than Two to Tango

We normally think of a relationship as involving two people. But once you begin to understand the nature of emotional systems, you recognize that it is just about impossible to regard relationships as involving only two people. Any two-person relationship exists within a network of other relationships. It is difficult for any two people to maintain a one-to-one relationship for any period of time. The more differentiated they are, the longer two people can maintain a one-to-one relationship with just each other, even in conflict, without distancing or bringing in a third party. But as anxiety increases, a one-to-one relationship is harder to maintain.

Triangles are created more frequently and cause greater damage when anxiety increases in a system. As a leader in the church, you need a good working knowledge of triangles to succeed in lowering your own level of anxiety and differentiating yourself within the emotional system. You need to be able to identify the triangles in the congregation that you are involved in and change your participation in them.

The concept of the triangle is one of the most important contributions of systems theory. This concept gives us a way to understand and even predict human emotional functioning within larger systems. It takes the attention away from the always murky world of personal motivation, why people behave as they do, and focuses on the actual functioning of people in relationships: who, how, what, when, and where. Answering these questions of fact keeps us from getting caught up in the confusing subjectivity and conjecture of motivation.

Understanding triangles helps us to see the individual within the context of the larger functional system. Once you become aware of triangles, you will see them everywhere in almost every aspect of your emotional life.

The Function of Triangles

Generally, triangles serve two purposes: (1) absorbing anxiety, and (2) covering over basic differences and conflicts in an emotional system. They keep the issues and the responsibilities fuzzy and confusing. This helps to keep anxiety at tolerable levels, as the anxiety is shifted around from one relationship to another through triangling.

Each triangle has three corners. Typically two corners are close and one is in the outside or more distant position, as in the diagram below:

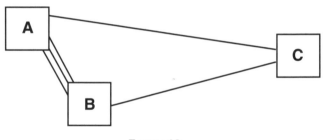

FIGURE 16

In relatively calm times, the two closer people will just make minor adjustments in the distance between them. They are comfortable enough in their closeness, and there is little anxiety to take outside of the relationship. When anxiety increases as more significant differences are exposed between them, either of the people in the closer twosome might become uncomfortable. The person who becomes the most uncomfortable first will make a move toward a third person. In the example above, Marie became uncomfortable with Harry's lack of response to her demands. She moved away from Harry toward Roy with her complaints about Harry. She wanted Roy to get Harry to shape up.

This often happens in marriages, when partner A goes to the pastor hoping that the pastor will make partner B more like A wants B to be. At that point, partner B is in the outside position, and partner A and the pastor are close.

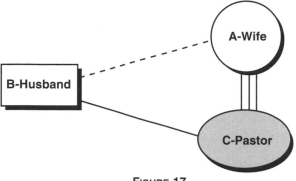

FIGURE 17

Or a different kind of triangle could be created if partner B becomes uncomfortable with partner A's efforts to change B and experiences a loss of self (engulfment). Partner B could then move toward outsider C with the hope of finding some respite from partner A's pursuit (or criticism). C may or may not welcome this move on B's part. If welcome, it becomes the typical "affair" triangle.

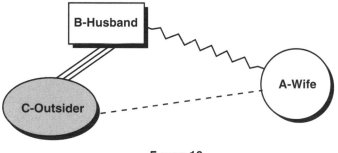

FIGURE 18

Another example might be a father who talks with his pastor about how to stop his son's drinking and get him to be a regular church attender. If the pastor agrees to help, they become the close twosome. The two of them could gang up on the son so much that the son becomes more upset, distances from them both, and begins to drink more. Two triangles then become evident. One triangle is:

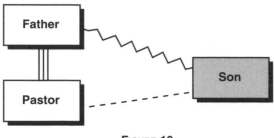

FIGURE 19

The other triangle, with the father and pastor together in the outside position is:

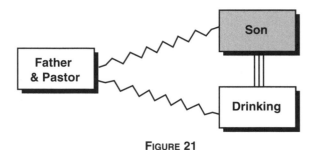

FIGURE 21

Sometimes, the more distant position is the more comfortable. For example, if mother and father are having an argument, one or both of them may try to triangle in a child. The child usually wants to be left out of it and keeps a distant position.

In periods of high stress and anxiety, people may try to get into the outside position, finding greater comfort in the distance. This usually involves people not taking responsibility for their own part in the issue and withdrawing or resigning. Roy certainly had fantasies of resigning and getting out of Valley View, as did many of the key members of the church. The church school superintendent, Maureen Niven, is a good example of this. As the worry about declining church school members built and her fear that she would be "blamed" for this increased, she felt the need to resolve the tension in this triangle by getting out of it entirely.

Movement within triangles occurs frequently; who is close and who is distant changes. This gives triangles their dynamic, and often dramatic, soap opera quality. And just like in soap operas, the more things appear to change, the more they stay the same. These shifts in closeness and distance between the various players of the triangle really represent no change at all. Change would mean getting out of the triangle, not taking part in the drama anymore but maintaining contact with all the parties involved.

Spotting the Triangles

Many triangles are obvious and easy to detect, but others, like the one between Roy, Marie, and Harry above, are hidden. Our best clue to their presence is our own sense of confusion. If you find yourself in a situation where things don't quite add up or something seems to be missing and the situation just doesn't make sense, think about triangles: who else or what else could be involved?

Another warning sign is when someone in your church talks to you in a negative way about someone else in the church and you have no particular "need to know." By getting this information, you might assume that you are now "on the inside" and a bit special. But keep in mind that the person talking to you about someone else is just as likely to talk to another person about you in a similar way.

Lolly McGuire, at Valley View, told her "friends" on the phone all about the argument between Stu and Roy that difficult Sunday morning. They acted interested in it and behaved in a friendly way toward her, as though they were members of the close twosomes in the triangles. But two of the people Lolly talked to, who didn't particularly like Lolly, told other friends about her "spreading rumors and gossip about the pastor," and so Lolly also became the focus of gossip triangles she did not know about.

Sarah, a member of Third Church, talked to pastor Bob Stimson one day about her negative feelings toward her husband. The way she did it was an attempt to pull Bob into the close twosome, putting her husband in the outside position. She praised Bob for his "sensitivity" as a male and for the fact that he was so caring.

Bob, however, was aware of the dangers of triangles and, unlike Roy with Marie, was able to state his position clearly within this triangle. Rather than talking with Sarah about her husband, Bob said what he would and would not do. He would either see her together with her husband (where any talk about the husband would be done in the husband's presence) or he would refer her to a trained pastoral counselor (who would have more experience in managing the triangles involved). By recognizing the presence of a triangle,

Bob was able to avoid endangering his pastoral relationship with Sarah and her husband and to avoid taking advantage of her vulnerability to meet his own needs, as Roy did with Marie.

Bob didn't make any comments about Sarah or about her husband one way or the other. He didn't take sides in her story or try to establish who was to blame for the marital difficulties. Nor did he fall for her flattery or blame her for her effort to develop a close emotional relationship with him. He knew that if he commiserated with her about her marital situation and acted like the caring and supportive person she believed him to be, she might feel good in the short run, but it would not be helpful to her (or him) in the long run. He would simply create a triangle that would make life more difficult and confusing for all of them.

Triangles may also be difficult to spot when they involve more than one person in each corner. Sometimes a group of people, a thing, or an issue can be in one or all of the three corners. In each church, the active triangles will be different at different times, but here are a few typical triangles in churches:

- the pastor/the choir director/the organist
- a church school teacher/a pupil/the pupil's parents
- a board chairperson/the pastor/the rest of the board
- a church congregation/the pastor/the denomination
- a church secretary/the pastor/an associate pastor
- the pastor/the pastor's spouse/one or more other church members
- two board members and a hot topic or issue
- the budget/the pro-missions money group/the pro-local church ministry group
- the budget/the stewardship committee/the church members
- the pastor/the building committee/the church building

INTERLOCKING TRIANGLES

Emotional systems are made up of the interaction of a number of interlocking triangles. Triangles rarely exist in isolation from the rest of the emotional system. Most triangles interconnect with other triangles in the system. As the anxiety level goes up in a system, more and more triangles will be recruited into the process in an attempt to get things settled down. We saw this happen at Valley View as Stu and Lolly called others and told them what was going on.

In the Roy/Stu/Larry triangle above, an interlocking triangle was Roy/Larry/Gene Lambert (Gene is Larry's uncle and a member of the building committee). Roy agreed to hire Larry as a favor to Gene. Roy felt a need for some support on the building committee (in his battles with Stu in particular), and Gene was a logical choice. Gene said some things about Larry to Roy that he had never said to Larry (who is twenty-five years old): "That boy is lacking direction. His father's divorce ten years ago was a bad thing for Larry; he never got over it. Actually, I think he's used it as a kind of excuse. But what he needs is a man who will take some interest in him, with a firm hand, and help him grow up to become a responsible young man."

When Roy begins to fail at what Gene hoped Roy would do for Larry, then Gene starts complaining to his wife Lata about both Roy and Larry. Lata might then talk to Larry's mother, with whom she still has contact, and tell her some of the stories and things that have been said. All of this will impact the way Larry's mother interacts with him, seeing him through other people's eyes. (Larry's problems also help her to continue to blame her former husband and carry her resentment about his "abandonment" of the family.)

Or Gene and Lata could talk with other members in the church and create a particular picture of Larry, so people give him more leeway on the job than they ought to because they now see him as a kind of "hard luck kid." But another member of the building committee may think they are being too easy on "the kid" and tell her husband how she sees it, and then he tells some other members, and before you know it a whole bunch of people are involved in Larry's life and taking positions that no one talks directly with him about. And then these others can begin to have the same arguments with each other that Roy and Stu and Gene have over how to deal with Larry and whether he should be the church custodian or not.

HOW TO HANDLE TRIANGLES BY REPOSITIONING

Movement and change in any one triangle creates change in all the others that are closely connected to it. Imagine that all of the points in a triangle are connected by rubber bands. When any two people move closer together, or further apart, the other relationships the two people are connected to will also be affected, as will the secondary and more remote relationships. Most movement in inter-locking triangles doesn't really change things in the system. Television soap operas go on and on—characters come and go, change places, keep and tell secrets, move closer and further away—but it all stays a big confusing mess. Nothing changes.

However, one kind of movement in an emotional system is beneficial to the system, as well as to the health of the people involved. This movement is to "reposition" oneself in the system. The soap opera story line would be over quickly if just one person decided to do this.

Repositioning (or detriangulating) involves behaving differently within the triangular process. While we may never get fully out of the triangles we are a part of, we can modify and limit our part in them to the extent that we can focus on just our part and do that differ-ently. Differentiating efforts will lead to repositioning within trian-gles and probably create a change that matters in the system.

For example, when pastor Bob Stimson used to go home to visit his parents, he would often end up alone with his mother. She would use these times to complain to Bob about his father. Bob was always uneasy with this and felt caught in something he really didn't want to be a part of. After he learned about the concept of triangles, he began to understand more clearly what was going on. He understood that his mother had difficulty dealing directly with her husband about her differences with him and that she used Bob to sound off to. This is how she dealt with her anxiety in her marriage. Bob had found that no matter what he did—arguing about the things his mother com-plained about, telling her what she ought to do, or just listening with-out saying anything—nothing really changed things.

Then he started asking his mother questions about her own thinking, feeling, wishes, and behavior with her husband when she told stories about him. By doing this, Bob became a resource to his mother. He didn't tell her what to do but stimulated her own thinking with his questions. By responding to her son's simple yet thought-provoking questions, Bob's mother began to take more responsibility for herself and became less focused on being a "vic-tim." She became more self-focused in her relationship with her husband and was able to think about how she wanted *to be with him,* rather than how she wanted *him to be.* She was happier, the relationship improved somewhat, and Bob had repositioned him-self in that triangle.

Bob discovered that by talking in this new way to his mother, they were developing a better relationship. She became more open about herself, and they discovered they had other things to talk about besides dad. Bob also started having a closer one-to-one relationship with his father.

The basic principle here is that one person cannot change the relationship between any two other people; efforts to do so usually only make things worse. If you are person C in the triangle, you can only manage your own relationship with either A or B. You cannot do anything about the relationship between A and B. As soon as you take a side in the triangle, regardless of the righteousness of the cause or of the issues involved, you automatically become a part of the problem.

Here is the story of one triangle in a church and the options for dealing with it. Paula has been the pastor in the church for just over a year. Penny has been the church secretary for fifteen years. Paula, unhappy with Penny's performance, frequently criticizes the quality of Penny's work (both to her and to others in the church).

Penny experiences the new pastor as too demanding, cold, and controlling. Because she is possibly facing the loss of her job or, at a minimum, the way she likes to do her job, Penny's anxiety level goes up, and she becomes more distant, resistant, and less open with Paula. Paula tries harder to get Penny to do things her way (pursuit) and only ends up more frustrated as Penny becomes less cooperative and less communicative. Paula begins to look for people on the board who agree with her about Penny, and Penny looks for people who agree with her.

This could easily become an issue around which all the leaders in the church line up on one side or the other, deciding who is "right" and who is "wrong." It is the kind of issue that much of the anxiety in the church could get focused on, with many interlocking triangles activated. But for the sake of simplicity (and things are never this simple in the church), I am going to keep the example restricted to just three people.

Feeling that she can't work the situation out with Paula, Penny goes to Marcia, the administrative committee chair, to complain about the new pastor. Penny and Marcia have known each other and have been friendly for fifteen years. This is what the triangle looks like now:

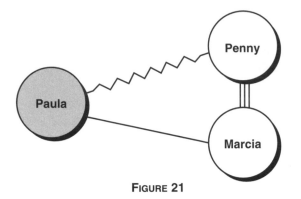

FIGURE 21

Up to this point, how things will turn out is still open, but this meeting can be the turning point. The situation could develop in a variety of negative or positive ways. Here are a few of many possibilities:

Negative Scenario 1. Marcia has also been unhappy with Paula's ministry in the church and sees Penny's complaints as an opportunity to move Paula out of the church (or to make trouble for her so that Paula might think about leaving). Marcia also wants to appear to be supportive to Penny, so they start spending time with each other telling horror stories about Paula.

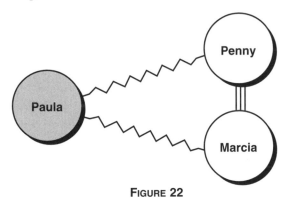

FIGURE 22

Over time, as Penny and Marcia complain to each other about Paula, Marcia, out of her own concerns about the way Penny does her job, begins to make comments about Penny to Paula. She is uncomfortable dealing directly with Penny. Things have calmed down between Penny and Paula by now but start to heat up between Penny and Marcia.

Eventually Penny stops getting together with Marcia and, because the atmosphere is calmer with Paula, starts to make somewhat negative comments about Marcia to Paula. Paula then responds with some of her own concerns about Marcia and talks about what a mess Marcia's personal life is. These two then become the closer points in the triangle based on apparent agreement about Marcia. Genuine closeness, of course, would be based on them talking about their own personal experiences, which they have never done.

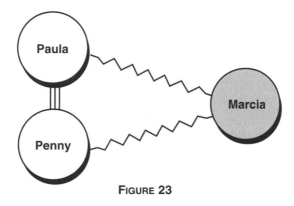

FIGURE 23

Negative Scenario 2. In the first conversation with Penny, Marcia takes the side of Paula and adds some of her own complaints about Penny's performance, which she has had for a long time. She says to Penny that others have seen her as uncooperative and just interested in building her own little kingdom around the church office. Penny then reacts, distances, and searches for someone who will agree with her about both Paula and Marcia.

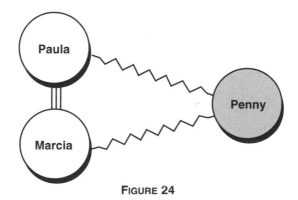

FIGURE 24

Both of the scenarios above involve people choosing sides. No matter whose side each person comes down on, she will be embroiled in a destructive triangle. Others will also become involved, and things will only become more difficult and upsetting in the church as a result. *This is guaranteed.*

There are also at least three positive scenarios for how things could go when Penny first approaches Marcia.

Positive Scenario 1. By not discussing Paula's behavior with Penny, Marcia implicitly declines Penny's invitation to form a triangular coalition. Instead, when Penny recounts a story about Paula, Marcia asks Penny how she dealt with Paula's behavior (as she experienced it). Marcia "implicitly declines" to be triangled in because it is usually not helpful to directly tell people, "You are triangling and I don't do that." This can have a kind of self-righteous quality to it, resulting in the other person feeling judged. Nothing will change.

People will justify their own position in a difficult relationship, as unclear and as un-thought-through as it may be, by telling negative stories about the other person. Telling the story is like saying, "What could anyone do with that? Don't you agree that person is unreasonable and is wrong, and that I am being hard done by?" People normally tend to leave out their part in the process as they tell the story.

Marcia helps by asking questions of Penny that help her to reflect on her own experience in the process: How does Penny understand Paula's behavior? Has Penny considered any other interpretations? Has she checked out her interpretation with Paula? Has she actually checked out what Paula means when she comments on her work? What keeps Penny from being more direct with Paula? How would Penny like to be with Paula, assuming Paula may not change? How could Penny approach this? What keeps Penny from doing that? How could Penny manage that part so she could deal with Paula in the way she'd like to? How might Paula respond if Penny did that? What would Penny do then? Are there any other options besides that? How clearly has Penny defined her picture of the job and her performance to Paula? Has Penny let Paula know what it is like to work with her?

There are hundreds of other questions that Marcia could ask. The point of the questions is to help Penny think about how she has been with Paula and her part in the process between them. This is not blaming her or making her responsible for all of the problems. It is just recognizing that she is responsible for how she manages her part in the difficulties. She is not responsible for how Paula acts with her. If Paula had complained to Marcia, then Marcia would ask the same kinds of questions of her. By doing this, Marcia becomes a resource to Paula, and helps her to discover abilities within herself for dealing with the difficult situation.

Even if it were possible, which it is not in this kind of triangle, for Marcia to step in and somehow change Paula's way of dealing with Penny, taking Penny's side in the dispute, such an "intervention" would not help Penny in the long run. It would keep her in a kind of victim position; it would keep Marcia involved for a long time, as each new difficulty arose, in something that is really not her business; and it would not give Paula a fair opportunity to deal with her part in the process herself.

Positive Scenario 2. Marcia shares some of her own personal experience in dealing with a boss who seemed less than friendly toward her, and talks about how she managed herself in relation to that boss. This would not work if Penny didn't want to hear about it, which would indicate that she may have some difficulty thinking about her part in the process. She can't learn from someone else's experience if she is not interested in reflecting on her own part in the interaction with Paula.

But if Penny is interested, Marcia can be a resource by telling about her own situation, what she experienced, what she thought about, how she felt, what she decided to do about it, and what the results were or what she learned from the experience. Penny can't do just what Marcia did because they are different people in different situations, but she can learn from hearing how someone else dealt with similar circumstances.

People often use their friendships in this way, to bounce their own difficult experiences off others, to find out what their experience has been in similar situations, and to learn what they have done about it. This offers new options for our thinking about our situation. In this way, friendships are resourceful. Friends rarely do us any good if they just agree with us and take our side in a difficult situation. While it might "feel good," this kind of support ultimately is not helpful.

Positive Scenario 3. Marcia offers to sponsor a meeting between Penny and Paula and to do her best as the chair. She makes sure that both sides can tell their stories as best as they can, so the other can hear what it is like for each person in the relationship. This option is tricky to do if there is not some spirit of goodwill between the two people. It is next to impossible if both people feel so unsafe that they are unable to listen to the other at all.

Other options are possible, but the point is that if Marcia allows herself to be drawn into the battle, either by taking sides or by trying to negotiate on behalf of one party, she probably will end up not being a help, and things will ultimately end badly.

TRIANGLES AND LEADERSHIP IN THE CHURCH

One of the greatest challenges you face as a leader in the church is that many church members will tend to not be direct and open with you. So, for example, if a member comes to you and tells you what "others" are saying, you won't know if that member is giving an accurate report or is just putting his or her thoughts into someone else's mouth to avoid telling you something directly.

In healthier relationship systems, people do not spend their time with each other focusing negatively on an absent third person. Instead, they work toward building one-to-one relationships between them. In a one-to-one relationship, the focus of conversation for each person is on his or her own self, life, and experiences, or about the mutual relationship between the two.

Triangles come about when people cannot work toward this one-to-one closeness and they don't know what to do with their anxiety. People have the illusion that they are getting along with each other when they are in agreement about the third point of the triangle, whether it is a child, the church, the pastor, the church school curriculum, God, and so forth. This helps them to avoid their real differences with each other.

Conversely, some people maintain a triangular relationship with each other by managing to be on the opposite side of every issue. They have a kind of closeness based on being opposites and never miss the opportunity to have an argument or debate. But their apparent openness is only about issues or their evaluation of other's personality, politics, faith, and the like. They manage to avoid any real openness about themselves and particularly about their vulnerabilities.

The story of the woman taken in adultery in John's Gospel is full of triangles. The primary one is Jesus, the Pharisees, and the woman. The Pharisees try to get Jesus to take a side so they can trap him. Jesus steps out of the triangle with his wise response to them, "Let him who is without sin cast the first stone." He directs their attention back to themselves and away from the triangular "other" focus.

There are no simple techniques for dealing with triangles. The basic and most important thing is to recognize their presence and to understand what they are about—what drives them and what is going on with people when they are in a triangle. (This is, of course, especially important if you find yourself actively triangling in the church.)

First, remember that triangles are normal. This is what people do with their anxiety.

Second, be clear about your own role in the process. For example, how have you created or participated in the pattern so that people can't say things to you directly? When people do speak directly, do you get highly defensive or attack them so they say to themselves, "I'm not going to take that risk anymore"? Or do you fail to model openness in important situations and show how a detriangulating style can work? Or do you somehow invite triangulation?

Third, since triangles are basically about people's level of anxiety, how could you contribute to a calmer, less anxious, and safer environment for people?

You will automatically become a resource to the church system and a leader in the church when you:

- learn to recognize these triangular patterns in relationships in the church and some of the underlying emotional difficulties that drive them,
- learn how to be more comfortable in triangles, less reactive, more focused and able to define your own beliefs and direction, and
- stay in emotional contact with the other involved people (perhaps asking the kinds of questions given above).

There is nothing better you could do.

QUESTIONS

For Your Own Thinking

1. In your normal daily conversation with others, how much time do you spend talking about people who are not present, rather than talking about yourself, the person you are with, or your relationship with each other?

2. How many "off limits" topics are there in your current important relationships? What topics specifically do you avoid with these people? Whom do you talk to instead about these topics, if anyone?

3. Whom do you feel most uncomfortable being direct with? What do you do with these feelings?

4. What triangles in your church are you aware of being in?

5. Do you have any ideas about how you could begin to "reposition" yourself in those triangles?

For Group Discussion

1. What are some particularly prominent or visible triangles in this church? What sort of anxieties might they be helping to keep underground?

2. Have you seen any examples of interlocking triangles in this church?

3. What questions do you have about the concept of triangles?

4. Has anyone in the group ever managed successfully to reposition himself or herself within a triangle? What was that like? What particular challenges did the person face? What seemed risky about it? What was the result?

5. What biblical stories or theological concepts seem to be related to the concept of triangles? Discuss, for example the Trinity from the point of view of triangles.

10

SIGNS OF SERIOUS PROBLEMS IN A CHURCH

And the man and his wife hid themselves from the presence of the LORD *God.* *(Genesis 3:8)*

"Miserable comforters are you all." *(Job 16:2)*

SYMPTOMS OF A CHURCH IN DIFFICULTY

All churches have difficult times. But the more fused the congregation, the more likelihood that it will develop serious, long lasting problems during these difficulties. Given enough stress and challenge, even better differentiated churches can experience a reduced level of flexibility. But highly fused churches quickly develop problems with only relatively small amounts of stress.

The lower the level of differentiation in a congregation, the greater will be the pressure on people to give up self and adapt to the functioning of others in the emotional system. The "oughts" and "shoulds" of others begin to run people's lives. Highly fused churches, like Valley View, will develop intense symptoms that can erupt over seemingly insignificant issues. And efforts to modify these symptoms simply by changing the minister, introducing new programs, working on better communication, or doing planning and goal setting, in and of themselves, will have little impact on the real problems. The level of chronic anxiety in these churches sabotages any efforts to modify the structure and processes.

Increased anxiety in an organization generally shows up in such things as members being consistently late for meetings or failing to show up at all; members being apathetic or frequently in conflict; patterns of illness or accidents; coalitions and cliques being formed; secrets being kept; patterns of functioning in which one person "does it all" or no one does much of anything.

There are a fairly large variety of specific ways things can go wrong in a congregation. The four reactive processes described in chapter 7 (compliance, rebellion, power struggle, and distance) were focused on smaller systems of maybe two to six people. However, the same processes can take over in larger systems like a congregation.

When a larger number of members compliantly accept what is offered them by the church, become rebelliously focused on church authorities, enter into a variety of types of power struggles, simply withdraw from the life of the church, or cut off entirely and move their membership elsewhere, these can all be symptoms of pervasive anxiety in the church system. Additionally, a large amount of intense triangulation, as described in chapter 9, can also indicate major difficulties in the larger system.

These symptoms do not represent different types of problems that need different solutions; they are all manifestations of higher levels of anxiety within the emotional system of the congregation. They reveal the lowered levels of flexibility common in more fused systems during times of challenge.

As one or more of these symptoms develop within a congregation, the anxiety in the system will get more and more focused on the symptom and trying to "fix" it or solve it in some way. This frequently has the opposite effect of intensifying the symptom, particularly when the specific people involved are focused upon as "the problem." This "problem-people" focus, or "other" focus, is a way of distracting individual members of the congregation from their own anxiety and conveniently allows them to point to the problem people as the issue that needs addressing.

Common to all of the symptoms is the process of emotional distancing. This pattern of emotional functioning during times of higher anxiety is universal and basic to human relationships. Each of the patterns involve, to a certain extent, the person hiding self from others, just as Adam and Eve hid themselves from God in the Garden of Eden, and from each other as well. We all know that anxiety drops with distance. As Adam discovered, however, even though distance is a good insulator from the experience of anxiety, it is not a good long-term solution.

One church board was surprised when a prominent member resigned suddenly from the church. She left behind a written list of grievances she had stored up over twenty years but had never discussed openly with anyone. She had kept her emotional distance from the congregation, even though she had been actively involved at the physical level. She had hidden her real self from them.

This chapter will describe three patterns (in addition to compliance, rebellion, power struggle, distance, and triangulation) that can be symptoms of serious problems in the emotional functioning of the church. They are over- and underfunctioning, projection to a third party, and impairment of a key leader.

OVER- AND UNDERFUNCTIONING

Overfunctioning happens when one person takes increasing amounts of responsibility for the functioning of one or more other people. Overfunctioners can take over the thinking, feeling, or actions of the underfunctioners. As the underfunctioner does less in one or more of these three areas, the overfunctioner does more. As a consequence, the overfunctioner looks more responsible, healthy, mature, and adequate, and the underfunctioner looks less so.

As children grow up, parents learn to stop doing things for the child that the child can do for self. The better differentiated parent acts on the belief that it is best for the child to do what he or she is capable of and to live with the consequences of his or her choices and decisions. The parent resists always rescuing the child, which shows respect for the child, teaches responsibility, and allows space for the child to begin to develop a more solid self. There is a time to lend a hand to a child learning to walk and a time to not take the child's hand. This has as much to do with the parent's anxiety about the child falling as with the child's desire and ability to walk.

There are times when it is also appropriate, and caring, to do for adults when they really cannot manage life for themselves. All of us have those times of needing others to be there for us, in either a material or emotional way. We need to be aware of others and of the kind of challenges they face in their lives, assess their competency to deal with those challenges, and then decide whether and how we will act in relation to them. So as Christians we want to be sensitive to those times when others are in genuine need so we can respond. But, it is uncaring and inappropriate to function consistently for others when they can manage for themselves, even if they want us to function for them and tell us we are "uncaring" if we don't.

For example, a pastor may be sensitive to the anxiety a committee chairperson feels about being able to do the job. She may agree, at his request, to sit in on a committee meeting. As the chair runs the meeting, the pastor sees that he is fumbling and uncertain. She may take on the role of the chair of the committee and effectively run the meeting.

Afterward, the chair may thank her for her help and ask her to come to the next meeting. She may then feel more valuable and important and gradually end up doing all the work of the chair. The chair, as the underfunctioner, doesn't have to face the anxiety of struggling to be more competent in his job, and the pastor, as over-functioner, doesn't have to face the anxiety of watching someone in a painful struggle in his work.

Of course, the over- and underfunctioning roles could be reversed, so that the lay leader takes more responsibility for functions that are really the pastor's. Some leaders in the church cover for their pastors a great deal, thus allowing them to be underfunctioners and not fulfill the responsibilities of their position. Lay leaders do this for each other on a regular basis, as well.

Overfunctioners tend to think they "know" what is best for others, and they often think they have better solutions for the dilemmas of others. While they often do have many competencies, the fact that their strength is used in the service of anxiety usually nullifies what can be useful in their abilities.

Underfunctioners will be slow to claim their competence in the presence of overfunctioners. They will tend to act as if they don't know how to do much of anything. It is easier just to be dependent and let others worry about our wants and seek ways to fulfill them for us. We can get angry at them when they fail to guess correctly about our needs, and this stimulates them to work harder on our behalf.

The church is famous for nurturing the over-/underfunctioning reciprocity. Normally in the church there is a small group of over-functioners, and the majority of the members are underfunction-ers. While overfunctioning is often regarded as the act of committed and caring leaders, it is not good for any of the parties. The more people overfunction in the church, the more all suffer from issues of confused responsibility. The clearer members and leaders can be about who is responsible for what, the better the congregation as a whole will function.

Overfunctioners can often see the dilemma they are in. But they try to address it in their characteristic way—by doing more. So typically they try to get underfunctioners to take more responsibility. They can get angry at them, feel sad, have breakdowns, plead, try to induce guilt, and try any number of other strategies aimed at getting the underfunctioners to take more responsibility. They don't realize that by focusing on trying to get others to be more responsible they are, in fact, taking even more responsibility. They are continuing to focus on others, rather than paying attention to just their own functioning.

Edwin Friedman, a Bowen theory therapist and pastoral counselor, has said that the issue for overfunctioners is not to delegate responsibility but to delegate anxiety. Anxiety can stimulate even underfunctioners to act (a positive function of anxiety). Overfunctioners too easily take on the anxiety that belongs to others. They have to learn how not to do this, or how to let the anxiety go when they have taken it on. Overfunctioners need to learn how to distinguish between what is their responsibility and what is the responsibility of others, and then they need to let go of things that they are not really responsible for. They can't make others more responsible, but they can make themselves less responsible. Then they need to learn to be comfortable with the anxiety they will have when other people do not do their job or do not do it according to the overfunctioner's standards.

Underfunctioners will take more responsibility and do their job only if and when they begin to feel anxious about it being done. They don't have to feel anxious about the job being done if somebody else deals with the job being done for them. In the church, if the underfunctioner has not raised his or her level of functioning even though no one is overfunctioning then maybe that person should not be in that position of leadership.

The concept of over- and underfunctioning can inform us as leaders, for example, as we deal with the issues of care and concern for others. A common misunderstanding of good "pastoral" care is that when someone is having a personal difficulty in the church, it is our job to "make them feel better." This is, however, a type of overfunctioning.

Because of this belief, many of us keep our distance from those who are suffering because we don't know what to say or do to *make others* feel better. Thus, what we primarily experience as a sense of inadequacy within ourselves is experienced by the one having difficulty as "lack of caring," because we don't make contact with them.

If we could let go of this more fused definition of caring, we might do a better job of expressing the caring we all do feel when a member of the congregation is suffering. Our responsibility is just to be there, to express the sense of connection we have with one another, whether others feel good or bad. It is not our job to take responsibility for the other's feelings—it is only our job to show our concern for and connection with them in the midst of their unhappiness.

In the book of Job, Job's friends thought their job was to make him feel better and to help him understand why his terrible tragedies happened. But their efforts became like empty words for Job, and he felt increasingly angry and depressed in their presence; they became part of his unhappiness. In their sense of responsibility for him, they *needed* him to feel better so they could feel adequate as caregivers. They began to see him as "resistant" to their help and became frustrated with him, rather than seeing how they provoked this "resistance."

Generally, words of encouragement and praise are good gifts to give one another, but such words are not always a good thing, even when we do happen to "make" others feel good. In some situations this "helpfulness" can increase the dependency of others and take away from their ability to be a resource to themselves. If a committee chair constantly needs the pastor to tell him he is doing a good job, then this dependency will get in the way of the chair identifying for himself what he thinks is a good job and will keep him performing just to get the praise of the pastor. He will not grow in his own ability to think or in his emotional autonomy.

And it is not necessarily a good thing if the pastor goes about always dispensing praise and compliments and telling people what they want to hear. He might so need to have people like him and to have a warm, positive connection with them that he is unable to provide leadership and to take difficult stands within the congregation. It was the fusion-based belief—that others are responsible for our emotional well-being and sense of safety and security—that lay behind most of the anger and blaming that went on at Valley View. People saw the pastor in particular as not taking good care of them (and he saw the board members as not taking good care of him). Who was responsible for what, or for whom, got very confused.

Another difficulty leaders in the church often experience in the church is stress. Stress is often equated with the amount of work a person has to do. Or we tend to think of it as related to type A behavior or to workaholism.

In fact, there are many very hard-working people who are very busy and who do not suffer any of the symptoms of stress. They function very well in spite of the number of things they are involved in.

From a family systems theory perspective, the "stressed out" experience is related to a person's functional position within the emotional system. In my clinical work, some of the most stressed clients have been those who heavily overfunctioned for others, often in a number of areas. One clinical researcher was unable to get any symptoms of stress in monkeys no matter how hard he made them work for their food. But shortly after he made one monkey responsible for whether others got fed or not, that monkey developed an ulcer.

People who regularly take responsibility for the functioning and well-being of others (rescuers) are the ones who often end up with a breakdown, physically or emotionally, or they burn out and have to drop out.

PROJECTION TO A THIRD PARTY

This symptom is a form of triangulation that often involves apparently well-functioning people trying to help or save someone who is not functioning well. The interesting aspect of this is that the more the "helpers" help, the more difficult the other person becomes.

The recipient of this "help" may be an individual or a group within the congregation at a lower level in the hierarchy, or people outside the church community who represent a mission for the church. A basic characteristic of this other party is the person's or group's apparent difficulty in functioning at the emotional, physical, or social level, which seems to require the helper's help.

One essential feature of this symptom is that several helpers—all of whom intend to help the same party—often have significant differences with each other, perhaps on a number of levels. They ignore these differences, however, by focusing on the even more different third party. This kind of triangular focus offers them the appearance of unity in their efforts to help the third party.

In this way then, anxiety within those who appear to be functioning well is ignored and transferred to a third party. For a variety of reasons, these third parties are often willing to absorb the anxiety and let themselves be the focus of help. They may do this happily, seeking and welcoming the help, or unhappily, fighting and resisting the help. But either way, their behavior seems to verify the need for the help.

In family therapy, it is common for parents to bring in a child or an adolescent about whom they have developed some concerns and who clearly seems to be having some difficulty managing his or her life. The more the parents have attempted to "help" the child, either by being more loving and accepting or by being more strict and by disciplining the child, the worse the child seems to get. The difficult child becomes a common concern for the parents and a focus of unity, so they appear to be working together. By focusing on the child, they are able to avoid dealing with any difficulties between them.

Church staff members can do this with another staff member who is not doing well in life. In one situation, a staff minister would regularly become the focus of concern whenever anxiety increased among the other ministers generally. He did have some significant difficulties in his life that they could all focus on and try to help him with. Some did this in so-called caring ways; others more angrily confronted him and attacked him for his "inadequate" behavior and his unwillingness to do anything about it. From time to time the two groups of staff would debate with each other about the "best" approach to take to help the troubled one, but both groups still focused on him.

Changing this pattern of functioning involved a process of getting the staff to identify a number of unresolved issues between them that they had a great deal of anxiety about and felt uncomfortable with. They were happy to distract themselves by focusing on the one minister's difficulties. As they were more willing to address their own areas of greater anxiety and developed more comfort in looking at themselves, the minister who was "the identified problem" on the staff started doing better in managing his own life.

In another church, an adult group made a project of helping a local community group composed of people who had been diagnosed as having "mental" problems of various sorts. The church adult group set out on a mission of "empowering" this group to better manage their own lives. The community group welcomed the church group's interest and efforts to help, for the most part, although some members of the group expressed resentment about this "paternalistic" help.

The church group became more involved in the life and activities of the community group, taking on huge amounts of responsibility for the various members' lives. At the same time, life in the community group became more difficult and tumultuous, and various members of the group became more dysfunctional or reactive. Eventually the members of the church group were overwhelmed by the problems of the community group. The more the church group did for them, the worse the community group became. Conflict then developed between the two groups.

Eventually the church group members learned more about managing their own anxiety when in contact with members of the community group and felt less need to act on their impulse to "help." They learned just to listen to the group about how they wanted to run their lives and relationships and asked interested questions (that weren't designed to change the group members). Then they found that there was some solid growth in the individuals. They also found that there were a few specific, concrete ways they could help, things the community group members were not able to do for themselves. But the biggest help came from simply being curious and interested while keeping their own level of anxiety and the resulting desire to "help" in check.

The community group members didn't always like this new way of being. They had their own anxiety about becoming more responsible for their lives, and they were used to having others move in and take responsibility for them. There was some anger at the church group members for not doing more to help. Community group members said things like "You've changed! You don't care about us anymore. If you cared, you wouldn't just leave this for us to deal with." The challenge for the church group was to stay thoughtful (which helped keep their anxiety at bay), to stay connected (rather than to distance from the accusations), and to keep clarifying for themselves what they were and were not responsible for.

Another way of projecting to a third party is to join forces with others to condemn someone or something that is regarded as bad. All kinds of causes and people have been identified by various churches in this kind of effort. The churches can be liberal or conservative; the type of politics involved are not the issue.

Racism is an excellent example of projection to a third party that is fueled by unrecognized anxiety and discomfort within oneself, as well as hatred for the other. By focusing on the different third party, whether a specific racial group or recent immigrants, people manage to avoid their own anxiety and underlying problems. Various types of white supremacist leaders (the first party) have been able to mobilize the fears of mostly poor whites (the second party) to fight against black people (the third party). This is the projection process at work on a large social scale.

IMPAIRMENT WITHIN KEY LEADERS

The dysfunction or impairment of key leaders in the church can be emotional, physical, or social in nature. A symptom like alcoholism could mean the drinking person has problems in all three aspects of his or her life.

The functioning of important leaders can be so tied into the church emotional system that their ability to manage their own lives becomes impaired as anxiety increases in the system. It is a fairly normal phenomenon for the anxiety present in a system to become settled on the leaders so that they become a focus of concern.

Churches do not "cause" their leaders to have mental breakdowns, to have heart attacks, or to steal money from the church. Many factors enter into the creation of this sort of phenomenon. However, the emotional process that a person is embedded in can be the source of enough anxiety to trigger the symptom.

The more leaders accept responsibility for anxiety that is not theirs, the greater the possibility that they themselves may become dysfunctional. Because the absorption of anxiety by one person produces, temporarily, a calming effect on the rest of the system, people unwittingly go along with this sort of pattern. Life is easier for them when the leader takes on their anxiety and seeks to alleviate it.

Often the impaired leader is in an overfunctioning position. One pastor, who was a major overfunctioner, had what he called a mental breakdown. He was put on paid leave for three months after being hospitalized for two weeks. His emotional life improved significantly during this time of rest, but within one month of being back on the job, he could feel the old emotional pressures building again.

In counseling, he discovered that the sources of anxiety in his life were many: ill, aged parents to care for; a younger brother who regularly sought help; and the many problems of the congregation. The church members thought he was a wonderful, caring pastor whose level of availability and sympathy seemed boundless. He had no personal life of his own, no friends who were peers, and no recreation.

But the breakdown did not relate to the number of hours he worked a week as much as to the amount of anxiety he absorbed from others through his overfunctioning. More and more people depended on him to be responsible for their well-being and functioning.

This pastor had to work hard to clarify what was and was not his responsibility and to develop a new way of relating to and caring for people who had difficulties. He worked at not taking on other people's jobs or doing things for committees that they could do themselves. He learned to be less concerned about things others were responsible for that were not done "perfectly" or according to his standards. He lowered some of his standards for himself, as well. He started taking two days off a week and did things that he had not enjoyed since he was a child.

As he became more differentiated within the congregation and his family and got clearer about the emotional boundaries between himself and others, he became a better pastor. He began to recognize how uncaring it was, in fact, to take over responsibility for others. He saw how that could rob people of their own growth challenges and opportunities for creative leadership.

It is fairly easy for pastors to become the overfunctioners within their congregations, which will eventually lead to some sort of impairment, but it can happen to lay leaders as well. Those leaders who are tempted to overfunction probably do it in the rest of their life as well (in their families, with friends, work, and other civic and volunteer activities), and the combination of so much overfunctioning in many different areas of life can lead to some sort of emotional, physical, or social impairment for them, as well.

The more differentiated a particular congregation or church system is, however, the fewer of these symptoms will emerge. The congregation will be comfortable with openly and directly facing the sources of anxiety and thinking through how to address them effectively. It will be less anxious about being anxious. Members will be more comfortable with differences, able to relate closely to one another even with these differences, and able to respond more fully, responsibly, competently, and cooperatively to God's call for their life and ministry.

QUESTIONS

For Your Own Thinking

1. How would you rate your own level of over- or underfunctioning compared to functioning responsibly for self and in relation to others?

2. Are there any ways you have participated in the projection process in your church?

3. Have you as a leader experienced any impairment of your own functioning at the emotional, physical, or social level? If so, do you see any connection between that and anxiety in your church? Does any of your experience of stress relate to a sense of responsibility for others?

4. When you experience expectations others in the church have of you, or when there are uncomfortable circumstances, to what extent do you use emotional distancing to deal with these?

5. Do you have any particularly good methods for getting others to distance from you? How might you typically get people to "back off" from you?

6. Have you ever taken the risk of being open and vulnerable in a situation where you were tempted to hide and keep your distance?

7. What conflicts with others are you involved in now? To what extent have you been able to identify your part in the difficulties and to be open about this?

8. Have you allowed yourself to take on the anxiety of others, making yourself responsible for something that is actually their responsibility? If so, how has this affected both you and them?

9. Are there ways you are allowing someone else to be responsible for things that are essentially your own responsibility?

For Group Discussion

1. These symptoms are about difficulties in the emotional functioning of congregations. Within that area, can you see how difficulties that have been present in your church fit with these?

2. What are the ways people keep emotional distance from one another in this congregation?

3. When people have cut off from and left this congregation, how have those remaining tended to understand the actions of those who have separated themselves? Have members blamed those who left or attempted to assess the level of emotional safety within the church?

4. In what ways has God been able to "perfect" the strength of this congregation through its weaknesses?

5. How have you seen the projection process at work in your congregation? What people, over the years, have been blamed or fingered as the "problem people" within or outside this church?

6. Have you seen any examples of people interrupting the projection process and of apparently well-functioning people dealing more with their own issues and anxiety?

7. Are there ways the anxiety of your congregation is getting focused on particular people, like the pastor, or some other leader in the church?

11

BIRTH ORDER AND LEADERSHIP STYLE

Now Esau hated Jacob.   *(Genesis 27:41)*

A woman named Martha received him into her house. And she had a sister called Mary.   *(Luke 10:38-39)*

BIRTH ORDER THEORY

A major factor affecting the way people exercise their leadership in congregations can be their birth order—their sibling position within their families of origin. Birth order theory helps explain why children in the same family are so different from one another. And it helps explain the variety of relationship and leadership styles that adults have in the church and elsewhere. For example, it is commonly understood that oldest children are natural born leaders. But, in fact, each of the birth order positions offers its own leadership qualities.

Psychologist Walter Toman studied many thousands of "normal" people in both Europe and the United States and identified a number of personality traits that commonly fit with the various birth order positions. This chapter is based on his research.

Birth order theory has much to say about our marriages, our way of parenting, who we have as friends, how these friendships develop, and even the kind of job we have and the way we do the job. However, this chapter describes only a few typical characteristics of the basic positions and what those characteristics may mean about leadership styles and involvement in the church. The characteristics of a particular person can be modified in many ways, so that a person may not look like a "typical" oldest, middle, or youngest—and no one entirely fits all the characteristics described here. But the descriptions given here are typical for these positions. (For more

144

detail, see *Birth Order and You* [Richardson and Richardson, Self-Counsel Press].)

These descriptions are not prescriptive; they do not say how people should be. They are descriptive, saying only how most people function in relation to others. For example, two coworkers whose personalities clash may have conflicting birth order positions (perhaps they are both eldest children). Understanding their difficulties from the perspective of birth order may help them modify their behavior with one another and work together more effectively.

The theory explains why some people, even though they are different in a number of ways, can work together so easily and comfortably. For example, an older brother of sisters and a younger sister of brothers will usually work together very well. They come from complementary birth order positions, and assuming they were relatively happy in their family of origin, they will be at ease with similar relationships at work.

One church staff group of six asked for help with what they called their frequent "power struggles" with one another. All of them were competent people in their own right, but each one also knew a better way for the other to do his or her job and, on occasion, moved in on the other's territory. They were a high-powered group with some outstanding accomplishments to their credit, but their conflicts were tearing them apart, and various members were threatening to leave their job if the conflicts continued.

It turned out that five of the staff members were eldest siblings who had functioned typically as respected, take-charge people in their families. They were able to get the job done, but it had to be done "my" way. The sixth staff member was a middle child. His frequent role in the staff was to rush from one conflict to another to put out the fires and "get communication opened up" again. His peace-keeping skills were developed in his family of origin, where he had created an identity for himself, quite typical for middle children, as a go-between person.

Each sibling position has its strengths, which help people accomplish their goals in the church, and each position has certain inherent liabilities. The hope is that people can enhance their natural strengths and grow beyond the limitations of their sibling position. As we work at becoming more differentiated, many of these limitations will automatically be addressed and modified.

OLDEST CHILDREN

These "natural-born leaders" grow up being comfortable exercising authority over others; they are often put into this position by their parents. They experience themselves as more knowledgeable and competent than their younger siblings and become used to the roles of leading, directing, guiding, and helping. This shapes their sense of themselves and inclines them to work harder at being capable and knowing more. They are usually highly "responsible" people.

The majority of American presidents have been either oldest male children or the only male child in their families. Only three have been youngest. Twenty-one of the first twenty-three United States astronauts were oldest or only children. In one study of twenty-five highly successful female corporate CEO's, all of them were eldest or only children (and none of them had brothers.) So eldest children are rewarded in our society for their conscientiousness and hard work.

But their sense of responsibility can also be a burden for them, and perhaps for others. They easily become workaholic, perfectionistic worriers. They are oppressed by the possibility that they might make a mistake, something that could feel "shameful" to them. While they don't usually show it, they are bothered by criticism. They can be tense, sober, serious, reserved, and conservative.

Others don't always enjoy being around oldest children, and this can make being an oldest a fairly lonely experience. They can often feel like the odd person out or never really a part of the group. They are valued for being able to get things done, but they are rarely the life of a party.

Oldest Sister of Sisters

This woman is usually seen as competent, strong, and having a mind of her own. It is not unusual for others to call her domineering, aggressive, and overpowering, although she finds these labels painful. She is not usually interested in either pleasing men or flattering their ego, unless the man happens to be a father figure for her. Then she will work hard to please him.

She may be strongly invested in looking after or nurturing those who are "under" her. She can be highly protective of them and can be firm with her exercise of discipline over them. She will think of her actions as being "for" them, exercised on their behalf and for their good, but the recipients may experience her as intrusive, nosey, dictatorial, and unhelpful.

In the church she will tend to the conservative side, uphold morality, support legitimate authority, and will tend to uphold the letter of the law, rather than the spirit. She may champion God fiercely but also believe deeply that God helps those who help themselves.

This has often been called the mother-superior, head-nurse, or school-principal position. More women in this position are in the professions today and are generally the ones "at the top." Another image might be that of Queen Victoria, who also happened to be the longest reigning monarch over England during its most prosperous times.

The oldest sister of sisters will serve God devoutly, and it would be difficult to oppose her when she "has God on her side." She keeps her finger on what is going on and expects people to be accountable.

Oldest Sister of Brothers

This woman shares the qualities of other oldest children but, compared to the oldest sister of sisters, she is more concerned about men. She willingly subverts her strength and competence to serve them and make them look good, even if she thinks of herself as a feminist. She will be comfortable with men, as they will be with her. The more brothers she has, the more comfortable she is around a number of men. They rely on her and think of her as a "good sport," always willing to pitch in. She is less tolerant of other women who do not understand this way of working and who want to be up in front themselves, or who attack "her" men.

In the church she is usually moderate in all things. She is sensitive to those who differ from her and believes in the value of mediation. She is comfortable with men in leadership but thinks that they should listen more to their wife who, if they were like her, would be a fountain of wisdom. Religion or theology is not her chief interest, but she will not be intimidated by it.

As a leader she is tactful, exercises care, works behind the scenes, and is a good delegator. Her efforts to guide others are subtle and gentle. The men she works with get the credit that is due to her, but she would never want to be seen as competing with them. She knows they couldn't do it without her. She creates an atmosphere conducive to good work. She is not easily discouraged and is one of the hardest workers in the church.

Oldest Brother of Brothers

This man is usually "the boss." He is a take-charge person. He wants to be good at what he does; he wants to win. Usually he is successful. He is not known for taking risks and is highly pragmatic. He is a bottom-line, just-the-facts person. Many military generals and corporate CEO's come from this sibling position.

He can be a tough, strict conservative, and others often feel misunderstood by him. Being close to others is not his specialty, but if he is close to someone, he will be close with men, rather than women, as long as they accept his lead, or his mentorship. He expects a lot from women but offers them little in return. He will tend to treat them like younger brothers.

In the church he often appears to be on the closest terms with God and, as God's agent, out to set the world right. He is interested in grand schemes and often quite involved in theology as an overarching framework. He is frequently the initiator of a new building campaign in the church, but this will be undertaken only if he is sure he can make it work.

He is usually seen as a good leader, if somewhat dictatorial. He says he believes in "strong" leadership. He loves to take responsibility for others and feels free to plan for others, knowing his is the best plan. He will want his church to be "the best" church and wants others to perform and fulfill this image.

Oldest Brother of Sisters

This man is more easygoing and less driven than the oldest brother of brothers. He is considerate, kind, tender, and less selfish. Many male gynecologists are from this sibling position.

He is good at managing relationships and can enjoy this. He gets along particularly well with women. He wants to see a good job done but not at all costs. "Live and let live" could be his relationship motto.

In the church, he is a moderate conservative with a strong dose of laissez faire. While certainly a competent intellectual, he also appreciates the aesthetic side of life. He does not commit himself to any "isms." He enjoys discussion, has opinions of his own, but has little need for fervent devotion to any set of beliefs.

He is normally viewed as a warm, paternal, caring leader. While open to becoming a leader, he believes the basic job of leadership is to let people live their own lives and to stay out of their way. He is a hard worker, responsible, and an easygoing superior. He is not easily discouraged by challenges.

YOUNGEST CHILDREN

The youngest child is the "baby" of the family, even if he or she happens to be seventy years old. Whether they like the term or not, they were the ones who got taken care of the longest and had little opportunity to be a caretaker. They were indulged (much more than the older children), and others tend to think of them as "cute" and "spoiled." It is hard for them to feel like they, and their ideas, are being taken seriously by peers or authorities.

Parental expectations of youngests often are lower than of the older siblings, so they experience less pressure to achieve. Their level of self-discipline could consequently also be lower, and they may be less decisive and clear about their direction in life. They may have alternating periods of being very dependent on others and then being quite rebellious against others, saying they don't need any help. The level of rebelliousness will depend partly on how much they were bossed around and teased by other siblings.

Being the youngest and the smallest, they found they couldn't get their way by exercising strength; they had to be more clever, studying others and becoming sneakier or manipulative to get their wants met. They know the value of either a pouting frown or a charming smile.

They don't normally gravitate to leadership positions, at least not as we normally think of leadership. If they do become leaders, it is more important to them that they be liked and admired by others than that others "obey" them. They are very sociable and popular among their peers, and they like to have fun. But if they were teased and made fun of in the family, they may be more shy and withdrawn.

Youngest Sister of Sisters

The perpetual youngest, she is spontaneous, happy, and something of an unconventional (for her family) risk-taker. She can be flirtatious, attractive, and play up her feminine side, but she can also be competitive. Enjoying change, she is erratic in her interests and involvements. Others might regard her as flighty and unpredictable.

Her competitive side may come out with women, where she is seen wanting to have more, sooner, of whatever is valued in her group of friends, be it marriage, children, material goods, or whatever. The more sisters she had, the more likely she is to be involved in activities with women than with men.

In the church she can have any sort of political or philosophical stance, as long as it is understood that she doesn't have to stay there. Generally she is on the side of change. Feelings will be more prominent than thinking in her beliefs. If she sticks to things, it could be as much because of stubbornness as conviction.

She desires the limelight of leadership but has difficulty carrying it off without significant support. Then she is easygoing and well-liked, happy to delegate and let others carry the ball. But she has difficulty making and sticking to her decisions. Her natural leadership abilities involve arousing a spirit of adventure, fun, and enthusiasm. For these reasons, she can be exciting to work with.

Youngest Sister of Brothers

This frequently attractive and fun-loving woman fits in easily with men. She often has many tomboyish traits. She appears independent and has many skills and capabilities, but she would not want to flaunt them.

In a man's world, life goes fairly easily for her, and many types of opportunities are available to her. It is harder for her to have a mind of her own if it could mean losing the friendship of men. She has respect for stronger men but is not invested in taking care of them.

In the church she is more conventional than the younger sister of sisters. She is not immediately upset with the patriarchal images of God or male leaders and often settles for finding favor in their sight.

She is more a good-natured follower than a leader. If she happens to find herself in a leadership position, she can do it, as long as she thinks others, particularly the men, approve of what she is doing. She is not focused on long-term goals because too many other good opportunities arise on the way. Her leadership comes out most strongly when she stands up for what is right and appropriate, in a simple, tactful, commonsense kind of way.

Youngest Brother of Brothers

This man is the adventurous rebel. Like the youngest sister of sisters, he is headstrong, unpredictable, erratic in feelings and performance. He is more a here-and-now person than a planner.

He doesn't like losing to others, although because of his lack of discipline, he may lose a fair amount. He doesn't like giving in to others, so if things don't go the way he wants, he may just drop out and leave the group entirely. Women are a puzzle to him, but they are drawn to him if they are willing to look after him. He is more comfortable around men but may be competitive with them; in this case, he is a hard worker. He needs an authority in his life to rebel against.

In the church he is not on the side of rules and regulations, and he is critical of those who are. He is rarely a consistent moralist. He believes people will get along if just left alone by those in charge. He gets along with those in authority if they like him best. He believes God will come to his aid when he has no idea what to do. Theologically he tends toward the mystical or the romantic vision, and he has difficulty putting his faith into words, or at least into words that make sense.

Drawn to power, he is not the natural leader his oldest brother is, and this often angers him and inspires him to fight those leaders by doing things his own way. In leadership he could appear unstable, unfair, and unwise. He needs older people to be his secret advisors and supporters without challenging him overtly. He leads the revolution but fails to guide the establishment of a new order. His positive qualities as a leader are his flexibility, and his ability to be a fresh visionary, bold, daring, and playful. When the times call for these qualities, he should flourish.

Youngest Brother of Sisters

Frequently doted on as a child, being both the youngest and unique as the only male, he has high self-esteem. Life does not require too much effort on his part; if it does, and he is not interested in the nature of the challenge, he will not take it on. Otherwise he is quite competent and capable of great accomplishments if he has a natural talent for a field. But he is regularly seduced by good fun and interesting relationships.

This man often finds himself in the company of women and taken care of by them. He takes this for granted. The women love him because he is so responsive to them and values their interest in him. He assumes they will look after the loose ends for him. Other men can become resentful and even critical of how much attention he gets.

In the church he is not highly opinionated and is open to any number of approaches, although he is conventional for the most part and has fewer doubts than others. The larger, global perspective does not interest him, and he is relatively less interested in other people's experience. If his natural bent is theology, then he excels in this area.

As a leader he is genial but not highly disciplined, systematic, or good with deadlines. He is better at being second in command and greasing the way socially. He works better with women than with men and needs the support of his elders (particularly females). He appreciates the talents of those below him. He shares many of the characteristics of youngest brother of brothers but is less reactive to and competitive with men. They, however, will not be as charmed by him as the women.

MIDDLE CHILDREN

The characteristics for middle children are not as easy to describe as for the other sibling positions. This is what they experience subjectively as well. They yearn for something that makes them as distinctive as the oldest or the youngest. Being a middle feels bland. If they grow up in a family that is focused on one of the other positions, the middle struggles more in life, wanting to have what "they" have. Life seems more unfair, and middle children set out to battle on behalf of justice (while, in fact, they are driven by envy of the prestige enjoyed by the eldest or the attention enjoyed by the youngest).

The middle child has the mixed characteristics of being an eldest (to those siblings below) and a youngest (to those above). While reading descriptions of sibling positions like this, middles feel left out. They fail to realize the advantages and flexibility their position gives them behaviorally.

Sibling groups divide into subgroups as the number of children increases. If four or more years separate those subgroups, a middle child is more clearly an eldest or a youngest within the subgroup, having both the advantages of that position plus the advantages of being a middle. Whichever child they were closer to growing up determines their own characteristics as an older or younger sibling.

If a middle's siblings are all the same sex, achieving a sense of identity is even harder. They are more likely to move away from their hometown and family in order to get a sense of self. One woman, the middle of five sisters, said she wanted to move to a city where no one else had her last name.

If the middle is the only one of his or her sex, he or she has a much greater sense of distinctiveness, and that person more clearly takes on the sibling characteristics of someone in his or her particular birth order. For example, the only boy with two older sisters and two younger sisters develops both the qualities of a younger brother of sisters and of an older brother of sisters. This offers him a greater diversity of experience to draw upon for his relationships as an adult.

In relationships, middles are great people to be around because of their flexibility. They can go either way as leaders or as followers. They are less caught up in the ego struggles of oldest and youngest children. They make good mediators in any group because it is easier for them to understand and relate to both sides of an issue.

As leaders they are more responsible than the youngest, but they have more difficulties commanding respect than the oldest, maybe even giving over their authority to an oldest in the group or getting caught up in a power struggle with the eldest.

THE ONLY CHILD

The characteristics of the only child swing toward either those of the oldest or the youngest, depending on both the nature of the relationship with the parents and the parents' own sibling positions. More than with the others, the sibling style of the parents (particularly the same sex parent) rubs off on the only.

Never displaced by succeeding children, only children usually have higher self-esteem. They do well with authorities and work to please them. They expect a lot of life and of themselves, like oldest children. They are usually successful at their endeavors and rate in the highest ranks academically. They may grow up too quickly and become serious before their time. They want to keep older people involved in their lives, as good friends and mentors, more than other sibling positions do.

Relationships are more difficult for them because they have never experienced the intimate give and take of life with a sibling. As adults it is a surprise to them that relationships are so complex. Being their own best friends, they may wonder if friendship is worth it. Social life does not have the same easy quality that it might for people who have siblings, so they get more anxious about things that others take for granted.

They are the ones who maintain the greatest emotional stability in a group, and their level of detachment is admired by others. They are simply above the fray, rarely getting caught up in rivalries. They are less comfortable working in teams and tend to want to have clearly demarcated boundaries.

Male Only Children

Given the continuing preferences of parents to have a boy, and of society generally for male leaders, male only children generally have it better than female only children. His life is the most charmed of any of the positions, provided his parents were appropriately admiring of him as their pride and joy and not too interfering with or too focused on him.

He is more likely to be a loner, and part of his work of differentiation will be to keep himself involved with others. He is not very interested in controlling others and is equally disinterested in taking care of them. Nor will he compete for attention the way others might; he will simply withdraw, saying to himself that it is too bad they don't see him for the prince he is.

In his involvement in the church and his leadership style, the sibling characteristics of his parents, especially the parent he was most intimately involved with, will predominate. The male only child frequently rises to leadership positions (because of his competence), but he is not always so sure what to do with the position or how to relate to others around it, and he is less understanding of the needs of those under him.

Female Only Children

The female only child feels very special within herself and is hurt if others fail to recognize her princesslike qualities. Most of the time others do. If she was overprotected as a child, she is more dependent than male only children for support and attention.

Otherwise, all that was said of only children above is true of her. However, growing up in a male-oriented world, she usually does not have as many advantages as the men and may achieve below the level of her generally high competence. She lacks the drive of oldest sisters—who have to work hard to hang on to their preeminence— or the competitiveness of younger sisters, so she does not seek leadership. However, when it is thrust upon her, because she is so competent she does a better job of leading than male only children. Growing up, she is more social than many male only children, understands better the complexities of relationships, and enters into this area with greater sensitivity. But she still wonders, along with the male only child, just how people can let their lives get so complicated.

TWINS

Twins are a world unto themselves. No one else can really understand what it is like to be a twin. This is most accentuated in female identical twins. Male identical twins seem to work harder at being different. Fraternal twins of different sexes may have the easiest time developing unique identities.

Twins will often become the "oldest" and the "youngest," even if they were born only five minutes apart. And, if they were not too separate from the rest of the siblings because of their twinship, they take on more normal sibling characteristics within the sibling group. The more central their experience of life as a twin, the less they may participate in group life, such as the church.

Twins do not excel academically for a number of reasons. They experience less push to achieve and think ambition is highly overrated, so they rarely seek out leadership positions. And because they less frequently develop the kind of competencies that might be valued in the church, they are rarely pushed into leadership. To the extent that their parents deemphasized the experience of twinship and did not emphasize their sameness, they may achieve and behave more like other siblings.

THE BIBLE AND SIBLING ISSUES IN THE CHURCH

One of the attractive and compelling things about biblical stories is how closely they reflect real life. Because of our own experience in sibling relationships, we automatically relate to the stories of Cain and Abel, Jacob and Esau, Joseph and his brothers, Moses and Aaron, and many other sibling relationships in the Bible.

It is not difficult to read between the lines in the story of Martha and Mary and to figure out who was older sister and who was younger. We can understand intuitively what the relationship must have been like between the two brothers in the parable of the prodigal son and how much their sibling experience influenced their personalities and provided an underlying dynamic for the strong feelings in the story.

Paul draws on the intensity and intimacy of the sibling relationship by calling members of the church "brothers and sisters in Christ." Some of the disciples were actually brothers, and one can imagine that when the Twelve began to argue over "who would be the greatest in the kingdom," this debate began with those brothers.

In the church, our characteristic leadership style related to sibling experience emerges and influences our relationships with others. When church boards identify the sibling position of each board member, they can usually see the link between each person's birth order and the stands they take on the board, the way they manage themselves with one another, and who they tend to get along with and who they disagree with the most.

Various congregations in a neighborhood, or a city, or even within a denomination may have a sibling quality in their institutional relationships. Much of the identity of a particular congregation may be in relationship to other congregations. Maybe this is true at a denominational level. For example, in the days following the Reformation, the Roman Catholic church was the older sibling against which other denominations attempted to define themselves.

Sibling relationships nearly always involve triangles. What occurred between Cain and Abel had to include the desire to please Jehovah. Martha and Mary were defining themselves not only in relation to each other but also to Jesus. Jacob's and Esau's struggles make sense only in the context of who got the blessing from their father. This story also includes the interlocking triangles with Isaac and Rebekah. Genesis 25–27 shows clearly how these triangles can affect sibling relationships.

Once we see how sibling position affects relationships in the church, we can think about people in a broader, more objective way. We can see that people are not just acting arbitrarily or irrationally but on the basis of what made sense in the context of their birth-order position. We can understand, for example, that a particular committee chair isn't being "dictatorial" in a vacuum but that the style of leadership comes with her sibling position as an older sister of sisters.

QUESTIONS

For Your Own Thinking

1. When people read sibling position descriptions, they often think their own description is off the mark, while that of others is fairly

accurate. Ask a few people close to you how well your birth order description fits you.

2. Which qualities or characteristics do you appreciate about your birth order position, and which ones would you like to grow beyond?

3. How would you describe your own way of leading, or your leadership characteristics, and how well does this fit with your birth-order description?

4. If there are some relationships you find difficult in the church, try to find out the sibling position of the other person. Does this help explain the difficulties the two of you have with each other?

5. Whom do you work best with in the church? How does the sibling position for each of you affect this?

For Group Discussion

1. As a group, identify your own birth-order positions and discuss what it was like for you to grow up in the position you did. What were the pros and cons of your own sibling experience? In what ways is your behavior in this group similar to your behavior in the family you grew up in?

2. How many oldest, youngest, middle, only, and twin children are there in your group? How does that affect the nature of the group experience for each of you?

3. Is there a sibling position quality to your congregation? What position style does it most closely resemble?

4. Take one of the biblical stories of siblings (for example, the Martha and Mary story, or that of the prodigal son) and discuss the story from the perspective of the different sibling relationships and what that might have been like for each of them.

5. Conflict between people sometimes has to do with the rank and sex of their sibling positions. An oldest sister of sisters and an oldest brother of brothers have both rank and sex conflicts. Each is used to being in charge and has less intimate knowledge of the opposite sex. Working together will be a bigger challenge for them. An oldest brother of sisters and a youngest sister of brothers have more complementary rank and sex and will more naturally work well together.

As a group, having identified your sibling positions with each other, discuss how you subjectively experience your working relationships with one another.

12

ASSESSING YOUR CONGREGATION'S EMOTIONAL SYSTEM

. . . that you may prove what is the will of God, what is good and acceptable and perfect.   *(Romans 12:2)*

But test the spirits to see whether they are of God.   *(1 John 4:1)*

INTRODUCTION TO ASSESSMENT

This chapter is only for those who are committed to understanding the emotional functioning of their congregation from a family systems theory perspective. The material covered here is too demanding and time-consuming for anyone who does not have a high level of interest and commitment. This assessment can be done either individually or in a small group.

If you decide to take on this task of assessment as part of a small group, it is *not* important that you all agree on how you assess the congregation. What is more important is that you openly share your best and most objective thinking with one another and that you be interested in one another's thinking. That way you will each be stimulated to do more of your own thinking and to sort through issues for yourself more clearly.

If you feel uncomfortable about "assessing" your congregation in this formal way, remember that we are doing assessment every time we seek to understand something, to persuade or offer to help others, and every time we hold a meeting to speak to an issue. These behaviors are based on some assessment of what is going on, what the problem is, or what needs to be addressed. We always make an assessment before we decide on a route of action. What is offered in this chapter is simply an effort to make this natural process more formal and more objective.

Assessing any emotional system is an ongoing process. Emotional issues may lay hidden for some time and only emerge in special times or particular circumstances of anxiety. And an assessment of any large system is difficult simply because of the complexity and the multiplicity of dynamics. However, it is possible to arrive at some understanding of the functional level of a congregation by studying its history and the present level of operating.

WHEN ASSESSMENT IS NEEDED AND HOW IT HELPS

The basic assumption I have been developing in this book is that emotional systems get in trouble and symptoms erupt as the result of some kind of imbalance in the system. The imbalance is almost always related to a heightened level of anxiety in the system. And anxiety affects the togetherness/individuality dynamic in which people and subunits in the system are trying to find a comfortable place for "self" in the community. The processes of fusion and differentiation determine how people go about doing this and, ultimately, how successful they will be.

If your church is symptomatic in some way, then it will be normal to try to understand what is going on. This chapter offers a way to get a handle on what is happening, without being too simplistic. Examples of a church system in difficulty include but are not limited to the following:

- A church is lifeless. It has no energy, no zest, no passion for enacting its understanding of what it means to be the church. It simply goes through the routines and has the appearance of life, but there is no creativity or liveliness. It lacks spirit.
- A church is always in turmoil and experiences an accumulation of unresolved conflicts. It seems to move from one conflict to another, or from one dramatic episode to another. The dialogue and the scenes seem similar, although the players and the content of issues may be different.
- Related to this is the church's lack of a clear direction or goals that are understood and cooperatively worked for by the majority of people in the congregation. The church spends more time being reactive than proactive, complaining about its past or present life rather than constructing its future.

- A church always seems to have a "problem" committee, or group, pastor, or other difficult leadership, say at the board level. In all other ways the church seems to be functioning well—except for these one or two "problems."
- A church is disconnected from or regularly at odds with its denomination in a bitter, angry way, rather than being involved itself with the denomination and proactively working to influence the direction of denominational decision making.
- A church experiences little sense of connection or community between its members, or members are unable to be open or real about who they are in the congregation. Connections cannot be maintained when there is difficulty or when something happens that might be considered shameful or wrong.
- A church does not support the development of mature individuality and diversity in thinking within its membership. It is narrowly dogmatic and excludes those who do not wholly subscribe to its particular creed.
- A church has no creed or clearly stated principles for which it exists and that it seeks to promote for the good of its members and society.
- A church seems to be an alien within its own social setting and deals with society with distance and hostility, rather than by being present, involved, and concerned about the needs of that society.

Remember that symptoms are not the problem; they simply say a problem exists in the way this congregation runs its life. A systemic focus will be lost quickly if the leadership decides to focus on "the problem," be it a person, a pastor, a small group, a committee, the choir, denominational leadership, or whatever.

Focusing on these symptoms, or any others, will probably prove fruitless because the difficulties lie within the emotional system of the congregation. Life would be wonderfully simple if we could treat emotional symptoms with programs and specific organizational strategies like goal setting or strategic planning, but unfortunately human beings don't work that way. These strategies are useful only if the emotional system of the congregation is functioning well.

One of the best things church leadership can do during difficult times is simply to understand the church better. During these times, simply achieving greater clarity about what is going on, based on the facts, will have a major impact. What is significant about this is not so much the conclusions one arrives at but the process of "trying to understand."

When leaders are able to adopt the "research stance," this style calms down the system. People are then able to think things through more clearly, be less reactive, and look at possible ways of doing things differently. More than this is needed during times of the highest levels of anxiety. At those times, the system needs leaders who will clearly and specifically define themselves and their own position within the system, while remaining well connected with all other key people in the system, particularly those who disagree with them. But even during these times, interest in the thinking of others will be a useful way of connecting.

The very process of asking people questions and trying to evoke their best thinking about what is going on will prove valuable. Just thinking about the questions and possible responses will help members (and you as leaders) get some distance from the emotionality of a situation and develop more objectivity. The assessment questions at the end of this chapter are not to be used with other people while the church is in the midst of significant emotional upheaval; they will seem irrelevant to the participants. But when things have calmed down some, people may find some of the questions useful and be gratified that you are interested in what they think.

GOALS AND PROCEDURES FOR ASSESSMENT

Evaluation of a congregation has the following goals:

1. to assess both the immediate and long-term factors contributing to increased anxiety in the congregational system; remember the bulk of the anxiety might be largely chronic and originate more in the history of the church than in present circumstances;
2. to define the main emotional patterns (symptoms) at work in the congregational system that are keeping it stuck or in a balance that is no longer appropriate;
3. to clarify what the basic level of differentiation in the congregation is so that the leadership might have realistic goals for growth and change;
4. to lay the groundwork for deciding how you (or each leader) want to be in order to create a different experience for yourself in the congregation.

Goal 1: Assessing the Sources of Anxiety

It is important, in fulfilling goal 1, to assess the present organizational stage of the congregation. Has the congregation gotten stuck in its development? Is it avoiding, out of anxiety about change, moving on to a new, more appropriate stage of development? What are the tasks and challenges for the leaders in moving to a new stage? What resources are already available and not used, or would have to be developed? One resource to help in thinking about this question might be *The Life Cycle of a Congregation* by Martin F. Saarinen (The Alban Institute). He offers some helpful ideas about the characteristics of churches at different stages of development.

What is the larger contextual situation of the church? The community it is located in? Its relationship to the larger social, economic, and political order? Its relationship to it own denomination? And to the surrounding churches in its area? To what extent is what is happening in the social context of the church affecting the level of anxiety within the church? How is all of this perceived by the leadership and the members of the church?

What sort of processes in the recent history of the church have led to the buildup of anxiety? Have any decisions been made (or not made) or directions taken that have not been adequately considered by the congregation and have therefore been left in an unresolved status? What events and behaviors immediately preceded the emergence of symptoms?

In this area it is important to be as thorough as possible in collecting factual data. Go over the life of the congregation for, say, the past two to three years. You'll need at least a small group of leaders, some calendars of church activities, and minutes of boards, committees, and of other relevant groups. Prepare a chronological list of "recent events" in the life of the church. This will give you a picture of changes in the congregational system in recent history.

Included in this list might be some notation of how the decisions or changes (or failure to make changes) were dealt with in various parts of the system. In what ways was the togetherness/individuality balance in the church challenged or changed as a result of these decisions? How did the leadership respond to the expression of anxiety in other parts of the church? Was it heard, adequately addressed, or ignored? Or did the leadership itself also become reactive? What came out of this total process?

Along with listing events in the congregation, you might include publicly known changes in the lives of the leaders of the congregation: births, deaths, marriages, retirements, divorces, promotions, or anything that could affect the status of important leaders in the church. Resignations from boards or committees or the addition of new people who have become influential in the life of the church would also be relevant. Who was most affected by these shifts and changes? How did they cope with it? What new behaviors, experiences, or shifts in congregational life resulted from these changes?

The danger in this process of data collection is to too quickly make assumptions, draw conclusions, and accept opinions ("Oh, that little change wasn't important") that will either ignore or tend to over- or underemphasize the significance of events, and to underplay the interconnectedness of events. The more specific and concrete you can be and the more factual you can keep the account (meaning free of evaluations about how important the change was), the more useful this recent history of the congregation, and the clearer your picture of the buildup of events.

When assessing the level of chronic anxiety, it is important to go back many years in the life of the congregation. A useful and highly informative exercise for the present leadership of the congregation would be to develop a "living history" of the church. This involves inviting the oldest members of the congregation to share their early memories of the church in front of present members.

This process can most effectively be done "fish bowl" style. The older members form an inner circle, and all other members sit in a larger circle outside the inner circle. There can be a facilitator who moderates the discussion, invites each older member to speak, stimulates discussion among them, and asks about people or events that have not been mentioned or that they seem hesitant to address.

It helps to have newsprint available, with dates already written on the paper, and then to fill in some particularly notable events in the early life of the church. Try to do a year by year chronology. The more specific about dates people can be, the better. These sessions can also be videotaped. An edited version of the tapes could be an important part of leadership training classes.

As the discussion in the inner circle becomes more current and reaches the years when people in the outer circle joined the church, then those people can move into the inner circle and talk about their early memories, being sure always to include in the discussion the perspectives of the older members. Former pastors, if they are avail-

able, could also be invited to be a part either of this process, or a separate event.

Questions to be addressed might include the following: What are
your earliest memories of this congregation? Why did you join this
church? What impressed you most about it? What was it like for you
to become more active in the church? What stands out for you, in
your experience of the church, as its most important turning points?
What unhappy events in our history seem to still be lingering in people's minds and seem unfinished, affecting our life as a community
today? What have been the best resources used by this congregation
to meet the challenges it faced (be as specific as possible)? What keeps
you involved with this congregation?

Some congregations have done this assessment as their only program for a weekend retreat, rediscovering many valuable experiences
that were a part of the history of the church. The exercise creates a
sense of connection between the participants, inspires many questions that people had never thought of, and usually makes people
prouder of the qualities of their own church community. It also
accords the true "elders" of the church a respected position in the
congregation. It will also reveal to what extent there may still be
unresolved issues from the past lingering in the church and affecting
the present emotional life.

Goal 2: Defining Symptomatic Patterns

When working on goal 2, it is important to remember the basic
reactive mechanisms (symptoms) for dealing with fusion in the
church: distance and/or silence, open conflict, triangulation or projection, and impairment of the physical, emotional, or social life of
key leaders. A congregation can use any or all of these as a way of trying to cope with anxiety. Have there been favorite or frequently used
symptoms in your congregation? What role do they play in the life
of the congregation? What has been the outcome of using these
mechanisms? As a group, discuss what symptomatic patterns you have
seen at work in your church.

Goal 3: Estimating the Basic Level of Differentiation

Arriving at goal 3 is the most difficult part of the assessment
process and must necessarily be impressionistic. It is deduced from
a composite picture of the data and based on an assessment of how
well or poorly the congregation has functioned over time.

One very basic point to clarify is to what extent, over the many years and events, congregational leaders showed an ability to separate emotional functioning from intellectual functioning, did not let emotional reactivity dictate decision making, and were able to adapt to reality and demonstrate flexibility in decison making. Clarity on this will help leaders develop realistic ideas about the possibilities of change in the congregation and how quickly or slowly it will come. Being realistic helps leaders raise their own level of patience.

It is also important when doing an assessment of the emotional history of the congregation to focus on what it has done well and what resources it has had at its disposal and made use of in difficult times, so that it was able to deal flexibly with events and circumstances when other churches might have folded or become more troubled. The point of an assessment, in other words, is not just to find problems but to also identify resources, strengths, and abilities. A greater ability to adapt to change and deal flexibly with challenge indicates a higher level of differentiation.

This last point needs some emphasis. It is much too easy to fall into a pathological focus on people and organizations. The assessment questions are open ended, they can help groups identify either strength or liabilities, so do not forget to inquire about the survival skills of the church.

Goal 4: Planning for Change in Self as a Leader

The point of goal 4 is to decide how you want to be in the church, given its history, the kind of emotional mechanisms that have been operative, the assessment you have made of the church's level of differentiation, and its ability to cope with your different behavior. So the focus of this goal is self, not others.

Any action that is focused on trying to change others or make them different will automatically fail and only lead to greater reactivity in the system. One can only be in charge of self, and changing self is more than enough challenge for any church leader.

If you are meeting together with other church leaders, the goal does not include how you as a group will behave. This is not a "we"-focused goal, but an "I"-focused goal. In fact, you may not even want to discuss with anyone what your own personal direction or effort at self-definition will be. The final chapter of this book, on the self of the leader, will describe some of the elements that might go into this self-defining process.

THE ASSESSMENT QUESTIONS

The assessment questions below are framed mostly in personal terms, asking about your own thinking with regard to the different areas. If they are tackled as part of a group experience, you could ask each other these questions, either as a whole group discussion or as a two-person exercise. If this assessment is done as part of a small group, various parts of the assessment could be assigned to different people, or different areas could be taken on by two or three people in a subgroup. But they are also good questions to ask of other people in the congregation.

If you decide to interview others in the congregation, be aware of issues of safety and trust for the members you talk to. You might have to make some decisions about anonymity and confidentiality, or get permission to repeat any personal information that is given. You might have to decide how you personally will handle the triangles that are made evident and to what extent you will be a party to secrets.

Some of the questions are clearly personal, and you may not want to discuss either your or other people's responses, or even to ask the questions of others. I suggest you let each person's own level of comfort and willingness to be open determine what you do and don't ask or discuss. There are no set guidelines, other than that you respect each person's limits; no one should ever be pushed to go beyond what he or she is comfortable with. If you happen to be discussing these questions with someone you do not know well, even if they appear to feel safe, you should check out with them their level of comfort.

The questions are meant to be examples of what could be asked, rather than an exact and exhaustive list. Many more questions could be asked, some other possibilities were provided at the end of previous chapters. You don't have to rigidly follow these specific questions; they just describe the territory of inquiry. New questions will suggest themselves as you allow your curiosity to develop in response to people's answers. Each person's response to a question should suggest five more questions to you. What is important lies in *thinking about* the questions, rather than in the questions themselves or the answers. If at the end of the process you end up with even more questions, then you have probably been doing the work of assessment correctly.

If you are interviewing other people in the congregation, then it is important that you not make the interview into a debate experience with them. If you begin to dispute facts with them or indicate to them that you think they are misguided or wrong, the point of this exercise is lost; one or both of you will become defensive and neither of you will learn.

It is not your job either to agree or to disagree with how others have experienced the church. Your job is to understand as well as you can their experience and how they have managed to understand and cope with events in the church as they do. If you find yourself becoming angry or even overly sympathetic with someone, you are probably caught in an emotional dynamic with this person and have lost the research stance. At all costs, you must not take this interview as an opportunity to "preach" to others about their roles and responsibilities in the church. While you may feel better voicing your beliefs, most likely the other person will distance from you in some way.

Each person you interview will have his or her own subjective experience of life in the church, particularly of what "the problems" are and what needs to be done about them. Blaming may be a prominent part of what others have to say. They may ask you to take a side, or you may be tempted to take sides in the stories they tell, but that will take you out of the researcher's stance, and the value of the exercise will be lost. The more you can stay in an objective position and invite the other person's objectivity (without blaming him or her for being subjective), the more useful the exercise will be.

The ability to think "systems" and not to get caught in an individualistic way of thinking will help you to stay more objective and calm as you listen to others and the way they make sense of things. If you find yourself getting anxious or feeling emotionally upset and unable to regain a calmer demeanor, it may be time either to change the subject or even to end the interview. You won't be able to learn from the other if you become anxious.

Congregational Emotional System Assessment Questions

Acute Anxiety

1. What are the "real" threats or challenges facing the congregation right now?
2. At what stage in its organizational life is the congregation?
3. At what stage are you (as a church leader) in your own profes-

sional, personal, and family life cycle development? What does this mean with regard to your own involvement in the church?

4. What is the status of the physical, emotional, and social health of the leaders of this congregation?

5. What changes are taking place within the organizational structure of the church? Of the denomination? Who seems to be most affected by these changes?

6. How are people involved with each other within the various congregational subsystems, and with those outside it? How would you describe the present state of the following relationships:

   a. You (as church leader) and your personal friends within the congregation?

   b. The governing board of the church and the church membership generally?

   c. The various significant subgroups within the church with other subgroups?

   d. You, your family, and the church?

   e. The church and its immediate neighborhood, and the larger community?

   f. The church and its regional and national administrative structures?

7. What are the main reactive patterns used in the congregation (compliance, rebellion, power struggle, distance) to keep things "in balance"?

8. How are organizational roles clarified and how is power exercised by you and by church leaders? Are people generally comfortable with this?

9. What particularly significant triangles and interlocking triangles are affecting the life and work of the congregation?

10. How do you participate in triangulation? How much do you initiate it, and to what extent are you able to interrupt it?

11. How would you assess your own level of reactivity within the congregation? How does it manifest itself?

12. What resources, skills, and experience does the congregation have available to it for coping more flexibly with these challenges?

13. What gets in the way of the congregation's ability to draw upon these resources?

14. Who (which individuals or groups) in the congregation, is most able to be in contact with the challenges, be the least anxious and reactive, and operate in a constructive manner?

15. On a scale of 1 to 10, how would you rate the level of threat people within the congregation feel (with 10 being the most threatened) about the "real" circumstances it faces?

Chronic Anxiety

1. What is the origin and earliest history of this particular church?
2. In the last fifty years of the church's life and development, are there any pastors, members, or events that have especially shaped the mythology of the church and its identity?
3. What have the relationships with previous pastors or paid staff leaders been like in the last thirty-five to forty years? Who were they? What were their periods of office? And how did things go for each of them while he or she was the pastor or a leader of the church? Under what circumstances did each leave the congregation? What was the impact of these "leavings" on the congregation? How was this dealt with, or was it dealt with?
4. What were the key events or experiences within the life of the congregation in the last ten years?
5. What other normal life cycle events or unexpected crises has the church either had to face or refused to grapple with in recent years?
6. How did you (or people) make it through that very difficult time in the life of the church? What do you think helped to keep it from being worse than it was? How come the whole place didn't just fold up at that point? What kind of strengths do you think people brought to that event so it turned out better than it might have?
7. How comfortable or anxious has the congregation been over the years? If one were to draw a time line, what would have been the more anxious and the more comfortable periods? Can you put specific dates on these periods? What in the life of the church did the anxiety or calmness seem to relate to?
8. How has "change" tended to happen over the years in this congregation?
9. What do you believe are the unresolved issues from the past that continue to affect the emotional life of this congregation, so things that are actually minor become big deals?
10. Generally speaking, how much difference does the congregation seem to be able to tolerate within its membership, and how comfortable can it be with differences?
11. To what extent are people in the congregation very dependent on others for their sense of well-being (needing to be praised by

important others or fearing their criticism), and to what extent do they bring their own sense of well-being with them into congregational life?

12. To what extent do people seem to be able to be openly, nondefensively a self with others, even if others are significantly different?

13. To what extent are people caught up in "demanding" what is fair or focusing on a "violation" of their rights within the congregation?

14. How much push is there for sameness and agreement within the congregation?

15. What subunits within the congregation (professional or pastoral staff, clerical and other staff, board, committees, programs, and the like) seem to be most sensitive (that is, think they are getting either too much oversight and being constrained, or think they are not getting enough involvement and support)?

16. To what degree are members of the congregation protecting anxiety—that is, anxiously focusing on what appears to be one problem area and ignoring other areas that may actually involve more difficulties?

17. To what extent are various parts or groups within the congregation focusing on the "wrongness" of others (and either trying to change the others, to win a competition with the others, or to keep their distance) and being either withdrawn or cut off from others?

18. How intense are the pursuit/distance patterns in the congregation?

19. Which people in the congregation are showing the greatest ability to reflect on their emotionality and to be more in charge of self while relating to others in the midst of anxious circumstances?

20. How many people believe the leadership has let them down or failed them, and how intense is this belief in the congregation?

21. How well are conflicts handled? What are the typical styles for dealing with conflict? What role do you tend to take?

22. What patterns, strengths, or sensitivities did you develop in your family of origin that are affecting the way you engage in church leadership now?

23. How much anxiety are you bringing into the church system from other systems—your work system? your family of origin? your

family of procreation? How do you see these other systems affecting how you are within this congregation?

24. How well can you connect with a broad variety of types of people in the church, and who are the people that you cannot do this with?

25. To what extent do you think you are taking charge of defining your identity and role within the congregation?

26. What particular skills and personal abilities do you need to develop to become a more competent leader within your congregation?

27. On a scale of 1 to 10, what is your assessment of the chronic level of anxiety in the congregation (with 10 being the highest level)?

13

BECOMING A BETTER LEADER

Peter said to [Jesus], "Even if I must die with you, I will not deny you." And so said all of the disciples.   *(Matthew 26:35)*

Paul, a servant of Jesus Christ, called to be an apostle, set apart for the gospel of God . . .   *(Romans 1:1)*

In 1 Corinthians 12:4–31, Paul speaks of each member as a unique part of the body of Christ and thus offers an organic view of leadership that is consistent with family systems theory as presented in this book. In this view, leadership is a part of the community and develops within the community. One can not cut off from the body and still be a leader. And each member of the body becomes a leader by becoming most fully itself, differentiating into what it was created to be. This means the member will be different from the other parts of the body while still functioning as part of the organic whole of the body.

In this passage Paul is thinking about the life of members of the Christian community in the same kind of systemic way that family systems theory does. Learning to think of the church as a system, one of many in your world, is the first essential step to becoming a better leader. The challenge is to think about one's own individual self within the context of community.

This chapter is about how you as an individual member of the church can use the material in this book personally to be a more effective church leader. Many books on leadership have been written. Generally they ask us to become something we are not and tend to say leadership is (in Paul's terms) like becoming a particular member of the body. The message in this book is that you become a leader by becoming more fully yourself, and by managing yourself (not others), within the context of your congregation.

The goals described here for developing yourself as a leader are easy to list and difficult to achieve. Working on this project can take a lifetime, but each small gain will lead to a better experience in the church for you and to improved functioning for the church as a whole. You should also find that life in general becomes more satisfying as you engage in this project.

Because most books on leadership don't recognize the extent to which organizations are emotional entities, they assume that if you get a leader who fulfills the requirements of the job description, all will be well. But when you think in a systems way, you know that functioning in an emotional system is more complicated than just fulfilling a job description. In addition to meeting the requirements of a particular position, effective leadership in emotional systems:

- provides a "less-anxious" presence
- works on differentiating a self within the congregation.

THE LESS ANXIOUS PRESENCE

The leader's main job, through his or her way of being in the congregation, is to create an emotional atmosphere in which greater calmness exists—to be a less anxious presence. "Knowing everything" is not necessary to be a healthy, competent leader. When you can be a less anxious presence, there is often enough experience and wisdom in the group for the group itself to figure out its own solutions to the challenges it faces. When a leader cannot contribute to this kind of atmosphere, the thinking processes in the group are short-circuited, and people become more anxious and more emotionally reactive and make poorer decisions.

A leader who is able to monitor his or her level of anxiety and who can keep that anxiety at a lower level than those in the group will have a significant calming effect upon the group. Improved functioning in the group does not always happen immediately, but continued contact over a period of time with a calmer, less anxious person seems to lend the group the ability to be more rational and thoughtful. With each new stage in the development of a crisis situation, anxiety in the group may build again, but if the leader can maintain a lower level of anxiety, the group may become functional again. Calmer churches usually have calmer leaders.

To attain this calmness requires us to understand better where, with whom, in what circumstances, and in what ways we become anxious (see the questions at the end of chapter 3, pages 51–52). Developing greater clarity about our own symptoms of anxiety and how we live them out within the system is critical to being more objective about the larger situation.

One major sign of being better differentiated is when we can be present in the midst of an emotional system in turmoil and actively relate to key people in the system while calmly maintaining a sense of our own direction. It is relatively easy to appear to be differentiated when the system is calm; the test is being able to maintain a calmer sense of self when the emotional environment deteriorates and life becomes more chaotic.

If the leader becomes as anxious as the group, it is less likely that the group will deal as well with a crisis. Note that the leader has to maintain active contact with the group during the crisis for this principle to be effective. It does not help an upset congregation for the leaders to stay in the office or the chapel and just pray about the situation. While the leaders are praying, the people will be reacting.

However, providing leadership in prayer *with* the congregation or the group involved has been one of the traditional ways people have provided a lower level of anxiety within the community. Prayer has a calming quality and encourages people to emotionally distance from a situation, to transcend it, and to think it through rather than just react.

Seeking to Understand

How you behave in contact with others in times of upset is important as well. When people are emotionally upset, it is not the time to argue with them or to preach to them or even to try to communicate your own point of view. The best way to have a calming effect on an anxious group is to be curious about how they think about the situation. This is done by asking questions and showing interest—by being the researcher, as described in Chapter 2.

Researchers bring a calm, quiet inquisitiveness that helps people in contact with them to think things through more clearly. Several psychology researchers have discovered quite accidentally that the people they did their research on made dramatic improvements in their personal lives in spite of the fact that the researchers were not intending to provide treatment; they were simply trying to understand the people better. When treatment programs were eventually developed on the basis of the research, those "treated" did not improve as much as the research group. Understanding people is more important than trying to do something to people, to "fix" them in some way.

The questions we ask have to be honest questions—not "don't you think . . ." questions, which have the conclusion built into them. The questions have to be based on the questioner's ignorance and genuine interest in knowing, rather than on the assumption that the questioner knows the right answer and is just waiting for the other person to guess it. Nor can the questions be used to lead someone to the questioner's point of view. (This kind of approach is sometimes called the Socratic method; it got Socrates killed. The Greeks saw him as clever and devious rather than as genuinely curious.)

Remember, questions that begin with who, where, when, what, and how are the most useful questions. ("Why" questions don't usually produce much useful information for understanding the functioning of emotional systems.) To ask helpful questions requires being aware of our ignorance of others. There is always more to learn about others. Systems tend to get stuck when their members think they already know one another and, in particular, what motivates others (why they do what they do). You can grow up with someone or live with him or her for fifty years and still not know the person fully. Healthy, alive, and creative systems are always more curious than they are knowledgeable.

Objectivity

Part of being able to be a less anxious presence is being able to be more objective. This is an act of caring. The person whose caring is anxious or more subjective has assumed too quickly that he or she understands what is happening and what people's motivations, intentions, and plans are. The person who offers this kind of caring knows what is right for others and what they need or want. This translates into overfunctioning and quickly creates either dependency or rebellion in others; it does not lead to true cooperation.

When we are being more objective, people will experience our interest in them as caring. While they may have some guardedness at first, if they believe you are just interested and not trying to do anything *to* them or to make them see the error of their ways, they will become less defensive and more open. Developing greater clarity about what is happening in a system will always be more productive in the long run than just having empathy for the "hurting" people in the system and trying to rescue them.

The mere appearance of objectivity, (that is, speaking in a calm rational voice, using logic, not showing any feelings, and so forth) is not a guarantee that someone is more objective. Apparent objectivity can be part of the emotional defenses of denial, intellectualization, justification, and rationalization. People who behave this way probably think of themselves as being quite rational, but they are using rationality to keep themselves emotionally distant from feelings and disconnected from others.

We are being more objective when we can be with people who are in pain, upset, angry, hurt, sad, fearful, and the like, and not need to keep ourselves distant from their feelings or to try to talk them out of their feelings (which is what Job's friends did with him). By simply being with people in their sorrow or pain or other upsetting feelings, we are demonstrating a deeper connection with them, and they will probably feel more cared for.

Lightness of Being

Another part of being a less anxious presence is having a certain "lightness" about the difficulties of the system. I do not mean "making light of" a situation, but too much heavy seriousness on our part means we are caught up in the system. Certainly difficulties in a church and people who might feel hurt or angry are serious issues, but being more objective enables us to put things in perspective. We have all probably told a humorous story about some painful experience in our lives so that people, including ourselves, could laugh, rather than cry, about it.

Comedy is partly about being more objective about the tragic experiences of life. Nearly any comic topic, viewed from another angle, could be seen as very serious. Humor is one of the ways we develop greater objectivity about life, as long as it is not used to avoid entirely any pain. Sarcasm is not humor; it is criticism and does not represent a new perspective on the situation. To be able to feel a lightness about a situation, rather than being weighed down by its gravity, gives us a less anxious presence.

SELF-DIFFERENTIATION

Moving the basic fusion/differentiation balance of the church toward greater differentiation is much longer-term work. Each member of a congregation will move at his or her own pace, and there is no way to speed the process up for them. But any movement toward differentiation by anyone in the congregation will have a positive impact on each of the other members in the church. Churches, and individual members, do not progress much further toward greater differentiation than do their leaders.

This means that the leaders of a congregation need to have some way of working at this process for themselves. This is not something you do for others. You do it for yourself, and a by-product is that others usually then do a better job of differentiating themselves.

The level of the differentiation of the leaders in the church is the crucial variable in how well that particular church will run its communal life, deal with the inevitable challenges and crises that come to it, and accomplish its mission. The goal of this work is for each leader to improve his or her own level of emotional functioning in relation to each other member of the congregation and particularly in relation to the other leaders.

This means developing our own personal model for how we would like to be generally in life and specifically within the emotional system of our church. This requires having a "self" focus rather than an "other" focus. We assume that others will continue to be as they are. Given that, our focus is on clarifying the beliefs, values, commitments, and life principles that make sense to us and that we want to uphold in our personal life and in how we are with others.

Obviously our faith is a major resource when we are developing a model for self. Our identity as members of the body of Christ will be reflected in this focus. But this faith/identity connection is a matter of more than just saying, for example, "I want to emulate the words of 1 Corinthians 13 in my life." Developing a model for self involves looking at this model in the specific context of any particularly difficult relationships we have in the church.

Note that having a self focus is different from being self-centered or selfish. A self focus allows us to be objective enough to develop a sense of our own responsibility and direction in the community. Self-centeredness is the failure to achieve this greater objectivity; it is subjective and keeps us at the center of what is happening, as if the purpose of life is all about us. And selfishness includes wanting others to be the way we want them to be; it does not respect the individuality of others.

Jesus, Paul, Peter, and other biblical leaders demonstrated a strong self focus. They were clear about their calling, their identity, their message, and their mission. Without being selfish or self-centered, they were able to focus on how they wanted to be in relation to others and did not rely on other people to tell them how to be. How they behaved as individual people was consistent, for the most part, with what they said they believed.

To function in a more differentiated way and lead the congregation toward greater differentiation, leaders need the attributes discussed below.

1. As a leader, you need an awareness of your own level of reactivity and the part that self plays in the emotional process in the church.

This means having the ability to step back from a situation and observe how you are affected emotionally, how you behave, how others react to your behavior, and so forth. To think systemically means to always include your self and your own role in an understanding of the emotional process. If, for example, there is someone in the congregation you are frequently in conflict with and who you tend to see as a "problem person," you might ask yourself, Do I know what I need to do to provoke that kind of behavior in that person?

One pastor, who described a board member as "exasperating," was asked what he had to do in order to feel exasperated. The pastor, bewildered, said he didn't do anything. He was just trying to get the board member to understand the situation better. The pastor was asked if he would experience exasperation if he weren't trying to get the board member to understand the situation the way he understood it. "Well, I guess not," said the pastor.

He was asked what it would be like to talk to the board member about the situation without trying to change her mind or get her agreement. "Where would that go? What's the point?" he said. Then the pastor was asked if he really understood the board member's position. He was sure he did, but when asked if the board member would agree that he did, he thought not. He was then asked if he thought the board member clearly understood her own position. He wasn't sure.

The consultant asked, "Well, how could you understand her position if she doesn't? What would happen between the two of you if you were really trying to understand her, rather than change her? If that happened, would you still label her as 'exasperating'? What new territory might be opened up for you as her pastor if you did this, and what new ideas might emerge about the situation?"

In this case, the pastor was able to pursue this approach with the board member. He found out a lot of things about the woman's background and how that related to the current upsetting situation and her approach to it. Both of them softened their positions enough that they found an area of agreement, a position they both could live with.

This skill assumes also that you have engaged in some effort to assess the emotional functioning of your congregation, as described in chapter 12. You must be aware in particular of the key triangles at work and how you participate in them.

The pastor became clearer about how his and the board member's relationship was affected by a couple of key triangles, and how a shift in his relationship with the board member would affect those triangles. He knew that both of them might feel some new pressures from others if they developed a more cooperative relationship.

2. As a leader, you need an ability to reduce your own level of emotional reactivity in the midst of difficult situations.

The pastor in the example above had to talk to himself quite a bit, both before the meeting with his board member and during the meeting, saying to himself, "Remember what you are after here is not to change her but to understand her. Don't take this personally." He also kept reminding himself of the larger situation in which the two of them played their parts. This helped him to keep from thinking the situation was all about him. This helped him keep calm, and he was able to resist becoming reactive and just to stay curious about what was going on with the board member and with himself.

By having a self focus (how he wanted to be in the relationship) rather than an other focus (how he wanted the board member to be with him), he did not react at the beginning of the conversation when the woman got into her typical way of talking about him and the issue.

3. As a leader, you need an ability to separate intellectual and emotional functioning and to not make decisions based on the emotional reactivity.

As discussed earlier (chapter 6), it is important to know what is a feeling and what is a thought, and not to mistake feelings for facts. Just because I feel rejected does not mean that you are rejecting me. I may have grown up in a family that was very uncomfortable with disagreement and made a point of agreeing in order to feel connected. So when you disagree with me, I might think you are trying to disconnect with me, when all you are doing is disagreeing with something, not rejecting me.

The ability to separate intellectual and emotional functioning allows me to clarify this emotional muddle. God has given us our brains to think through these issues in which we tend to get muddled up emotionally. It is one of our most important resources, and leaders need to develop their own thinking abilities and help others to think. If the leaders of a congregation begin to invest in this work, others will learn from it and may be more willing to do it themselves. As a result, the general level of differentiation in the congregation will increase.

4. As a leader, you need an ability to act on the basis of your principled beliefs in a way that is consistent with your goals.

Emotional systems attempt to keep their members at a particular place and fulfilling a certain role in the mobile. As anxiety goes up in the system, this pressure intensifies. A differentiating act, when you move in an unexpected way within the congregation, will probably elicit more anxiety. This action requires that you have a clear focus on where you are heading and that you not let yourself get distracted by reactivity to others.

There is a kind of personal anxiety that goes with a differentiating act. You are going into new territory, into the unknown, and it is normal to have some anxiety about this. But keeping the focus on how you want to be will help you with this experience.

PREPARING FOR THE REACTION

Differentiating yourself within the group often does not lead to praise from the group but to a negative reaction at first. This reaction is related to the challenge people experience when someone takes a new position within the emotional system. Your new position has an unbalancing effect on the group mobile. It may "feel" wrong to those close to you, and they will react, saying that you are wrong or bad or crazy and that you must change back to how you used to be.

Your efforts to differentiate within the emotional system of the congregation need to include an assessment of what triangles might be stimulated and how various people will respond. You need to make plans about how you will manage yourself in the midst of their reactions. It is essential at the point of their reaction to not react personally yourself to their reactions. If you do, nothing will change. The point is to maintain your own direction while also doing your part to maintain the connection with others, nonreactively.

Even friendly and supportive reactions can be a problem. While it may feel good, this can be a prelude to the development of camps or polarized positions, which will mean no change has happened. The process of differentiating is not to get support, and supportive responses from others can inhibit the impact of the work. The best response is when others work more at defining themselves rather than joining "your side."

When Jesus told the disciples his mission included going to Jerusalem and being killed and that they would abandon him, they reacted by telling him he was wrong and that it wasn't going to be that way. But his self-definition did not need their cooperation or agreement or even their understanding. They did abandon him when he was arrested and crucified.

When Paul confronted the rest of the church leaders in Jerusalem and told them the gospel was much larger than they had suspected, that God had done something totally new through Jesus and that he (Paul) was going to evangelize Gentiles without asking them first to become Jews (through circumcision), the other church leaders told him he was wrong (and possibly immoral).

Paul went ahead with his mission in the Gentile world mostly without full understanding or support of the church's leaders. However, he maintained his connections with the church in Israel and did not let the significant differences they had with each other get in the way of his sense of connection with them. He demonstrated this connection materially by taking offerings from the Gentile churches to help support the church in Jerusalem.

Neither Jesus nor Paul cut off from those people who disagreed with them. The disciples and the church leaders distanced from Jesus and Paul, but Jesus and Paul did not let themselves be overcome with feelings of abandonment (although they must have felt bad) or become reactive to the reactivity of the others. They maintained their side of the connection and got on with their understanding of their mission. Eventually the church joined them at a new level of functioning.

CONCLUSION

Working on one's own level of differentiation is not about salvation. Salvation is not something we do anything to achieve; it is a free gift based on God's grace and love for us. It is not based on any act of ours, and being either more fused or more differentiated does not affect, in the slightest way, God's stance toward us.

Becoming a more differentiated self might be included in our concept of sanctification. This is a process through which we more and more take on the nature of Christ through the active presence of God's Holy Spirit. This requires our participation, or "working out your own salvation," for it is God at work within us (Phil. 2:12-13). This process of realizing one's salvation by God, of more actively being a member of Christ's body in the world, is vastly strengthened by one's ability to be a more differentiated self.

So differentiation may be considered a requirement for our own spiritual growth as Christians. We may have essentially "correct beliefs," but without the ability to be more differentiated, we will not be able to act consistently on these beliefs. The better differentiated we are, the more we can behave in ways consistent with our own professed beliefs.

Murray Bowen, who was not a religious man, once said it would be hard to find a better definition of differentiation than the prayer of St. Francis of Assisi:

Lord, make me an instrument of your peace;
Where there is hatred, let me sow love;
Where there is injury, pardon;
Where there is doubt, faith;
Where there is despair, hope;
Where there is darkness, light, and
Where there is sadness, joy.

O Divine Master,
Grant that I may not so much
Seek to be consoled as to console;
To be understood as to understand;
To be loved as to love;
For it is in giving that we receive;
It is in pardoning that we are pardoned;
And, it is in dying that we are born to eternal life.

On another occasion, addressing a group of religious leaders, Bowen said:

A major quality in the differentiation of self is complete selflessness in which "doing for others" replaces selfish personal goals. Jesus Christ has been a model of total selflessness. . . . A well differentiated self has to get beyond the selfish promotion of self. One has always to be aware of "the other."

"Selflessness" does not mean "no-self" but the ability to have a larger, more objective view of things, where self is not at the center. In other words, differentiation is a way to humility, as well as to wisdom.

BIBLIOGRAPHY

If you wish to do further reading in Bowen Family Systems Theory, here are a few suggestions.

Bowen, Murray.
1978   *Family Therapy in Clinical Practice.* New York: Jason Aronson, Inc.

Friedman, Edwin H.
1985   *Generation to Generation: Family Process in Church and Synagogue.* New York: The Guildford Press.

Gilbert, Roberta M.
1992   *Extraordinary Relationships: A New Way of Thinking About Human Interactions.* Minneapolis: Chronimed Publishing.

Kerr, Michael E., and Bowen, Murray.
1988   *Family Evaulation: The Role of Family as an Emotional Unit that Governs Individual Behavior and Development.* New York: W. W. Norton and Co.

Kiley, Ruth, and Wiseman, Kathleen Klaus.
1982   *Understanding Organizations: Application of Bowen Family Systems Theory.* Washington, D.C.: The Georgetown University Family Center.

Papero, Daniel V.
1992   *Bowen Family Systems Theory.* Boston: Allyn and Bacon.

Richardson, Lois, and Richardson, Ronald W.
1990   *Birth Order and You: How Your Sex and Position in the Family Affects your Personality and Relationships.* Vancouver: Self-Counsel Press.

Richardson, Ronald W.
1984   *Family Ties That Bind: A Self-Help Guide to Change through Family of Origin Therapy.* Vancouver: Self-Counsel Press.